Labour Camp

Camp is the consistently aesthetic experience of the world. It incarnates a victory of 'style' over 'content', 'aesthetics' over 'morality', of irony over tragedy.
Susan Sontag, *Notes on Camp*, 1964

a politician is an arse upon which everyone has sat except a man.
eecummings, *1 x 1*, 1947

Labour Camp

The failure of style over substance

STEPHEN BAYLEY

B T Batsford Ltd · London

Acknowledgement

This book was Naomi Roth's idea. She had the wit to ask for it, the patience to edit it and the nerve to publish it.

First published in 1998 by
B. T. Batsford Ltd
583 Fulham Road London SW6 5BY

A catalogue record for this book is available from the British Library.

ISBN 0 7134 8479 9

Designed by DWN Ltd, London
Typeset by Kenneth Burnley, Wirral, Cheshire
Printed in Great Britain by
Redwood Books, Trowbridge, Wilts

Batsford OnLine: http://www.batsford.com

Contents

The Prime Minister Goes for a Spin

'The sight of the Blairs actually arriving at Downing Street in a forlorn Montego Estate was – depending on the colour of your point of view – as cruelly disillusioning or as neatly confirming of prejudice as Prescott wearing a gorilla costume and swinging a football rattle at his first Cabinet meeting.'

All life, according to Nietzsche, is a question of taste. And he was right. And so was Susan Sontag who wrote in her 1964 essay 'Notes on Camp' that 'Taste governs every free – as opposed to rote – human response.' It was in this same essay that she convincingly proposed a definition of 'Camp' as style-over-content. As a criticism, this trope has dominated comment about the New Labour Government since its election victory in May 1997.

The fascination of the modern world is that the realm of aesthetics does not end at the doors of the Tate Gallery. Art and advertising, commerce and culture have become one. Some might add politics to that list. Industrial design is our folk art. In this game there is no standing on the sideline, no such thing as a value-free decision not to be involved. And cars, being invested with more 'design' than any other commodity, are cruelly revealing of our tastes. 'I don't care about cars, I just drive an old Montego' is a testament of faith. It means you care about cars rather a lot really.

I'd had Tony Blair down for a SAAB, a car that's intelligent, responsible, non-aggressive, but also just a teeny bit raffish. No slam dunk of testosterone here: these cars are gender-free. Provincial solicitors might drive steady Volvos, but urban barristers prefer slinkier SAABs, cars with a high IQ. The parallels between the GAP-clad, Oddbins-quaffing Blair – or perhaps I mean the *image* of Blair – and the eco-sensitive SAAB are surprising. Like Blair, the SAAB 900 looks good, and appears to be the quintessence of social democracy, but underneath it has a dark secret. It's nothing more than a very ordinary old-regime Vauxhall Cavalier dressed in impressive new(ish) clothes.

So the Prime Minister's arrival at church on one of his very first public outings in a Ford Galaxy was something of a surprise. It's certain that Blair's courtiers had taken the iconography of this one very seriously indeed. The Galaxy is the most successful of the new category of MPVs (Multi Purpose Vehicles). It's not just a new car: it is a new *type* of car – and here, of course, is its significance.

Given the Prime Minister's domestic obligations and arrangements, he could have chosen an estate car, but that would have excited too many associations with cosy suburbia. A Range Rover would have done the job, but that would have been too much Mr and Mrs Deposed-Tory of Cirencester and with lots of ineffable rural associations, upsetting to the anti-hunt and tree-hugging lobby. A luxury car, on the other hand – a Jaguar perhaps – was too undemocratic: but a people-mover seemed just right, the sort of car politicians can hold talks in, move people, that sort of thing. The symmetry was marvellous.

Never mind that to many people the styling of the Galaxy gives an unusual impression that the car might, at any one time, be coming or going. Never mind that it can't decide whether it's a minibus or a sports car. Never mind either that the capacity to accommodate so many fellow-travellers seems at odds with the principles of freedom and independence which are the source of the motoring bug. The Galaxy's other attributes provide a perfect iconographic system for New Labour. It's sophisticated, mature (but not old-fart), outgoing and as flexible in its accommodation as New Labour is in its policy. And of course, it's European. This Ford is not made in Dagenham or Halewood, but in a joint venture with Volkswagen at a new site in Portugal. If the Galaxy were a person it would be a forty-ish graduate, given to wearing deck shoes (probably with socks) at weekends, buying wine at Oddbins, chinos from Gap and possessing committed views on child-rearing, forests and Third-World debt.

The Galaxy is New Labour on wheels . . . or, at least, in theory. If the sight of a brand-new, delivery-mileage-only Prime Minister driving himself to church in a Postmodern monospace seven-seat V6 people-mover was a surprise, the sight of the Blairs *actually* arriving at Downing Street (when a formal photo opportunity had not been announced) in a forlorn Montego Estate was – depending on the colour of your prejudices – as cruelly disillusioning or as neatly confirming some prejudices as Prescott wearing a gorilla costume and swinging a football rattle at his first cabinet meeting. For this melancholy device is the Blairs' private car, and it is irresistibly tempting to make the telling comparison of Chardonnay/brown ale, New Labour/old Labour and Galaxy/Montego. And very depressing it is.

Television news showed the Montego missing a plastic hubcap – telltale slovenliness – on a course of automatic physical disintegration to complement the necessary intellectual deconstruction demanded by the Blairs' consumer choice. The Montego is a survivor of the pre-anaesthetic days of the British car industry when the British car industry was still British. It is a vehicle entirely without personal charm or capability and with so little technical merit that only the most sensitive instruments could detect it. It was manufactured to a price rather than to a standard. Great designs are an expression of belief. Great designs have a moral quality. The Montego was not a great design.

The production technology employed to manufacture it was so backward and full of redundant processes and wanton complexity that mediocre quality and unreliability were standard fittings, along with interior design using Iron Curtain plastics and the aesthetics of a Romanian psychiatric hospital. They couldn't work out how to impregnate the bumpers with body colour so they had to paint them. Engines were crude and interior design reminiscent of the Polish avant-garde of the 1970s: lots of daring angles and glossy plastic and depressing tilts at modernism. As a driver's car, a Montego is no more stimulating than an afternoon in a day-care centre, its handling like a hospital gurney missing a wheel. It is the utter negation of joy, optimism, positivism and a sense of progress. It is depression made visible: dispiriting, cynical, ugly, backward and despairing. It is the Blairs' personal choice. Someone capable of tolerating such awfulness is not to be trusted. But, of course, this was the off-camera reality, as opposed to the photo-opportunity.

Will we see Ministers all in Galaxys one day, opportunistically fiddling with swivelling conference chairs so as to change direction with the ebb and flow of public opinion? Among all its many merits, the Galaxy is one of the few cars you can buy which allows passengers to sit with their backs to the direction of progress. Since it cannot easily be classified, it's a fine car for politicians. But even if Ford's popular people-mover does not officially replace the ageing fleet of government Rovers, one thing is certain: the choice of private car should be on the declaration of members' interests.

Foreword

We have 'New Labour' and, any minute now – sometime around
the Millennium, one suspects – we will have 'New Britain'. It's a
tired old joke in the advertising world that if you don't have anything
to say about a product, the words 'New', 'You' and 'Free' are
guaranteed to get the consumer's attention.

What is New Britain actually going to be like? One thousand years
ago we were locked in tense and timorous expectation of the
Apocalypse. Our own millenarian obsession is with image, style and
national identity. I think you can forget about Betjeman's village
green as a model, as much as you can forget about the alternative
vision, which the Poet Laureate so reviled, of a Britain full of council
blocks and by-passes. Something else – a weird brew of advertising
sensibilities, image-manipulation and spin – is being prepared by the
extraordinary Peter Mandelson in his Ministry of Soundbites.

Not since the elaborate refinements of Byzantium has a civilization
cared so much about the nuances of iconography, the heraldry of
nationhood. This obsession with style may be *the* distinctive
feature of our *fin-de-siècle*. Harold Macmillan cared so little for the
look and taste of things that he thought it was ungentlemanly
actually to notice what was on his plate. Yet one imagines that *The
River Café Cookbook* is more prominent in Tony Blair's library than
Walter Bagehot or John Ruskin. In New Britain the Stones of
Venice might be mistaken for a new north Italian polenta dish.
Probably *seared.*

The Millennium hits the peak of the third great age of human economic activity. The first stage in the long journey from the primeval glop was achieved when wealth (and therefore power) was derived from possession of land and natural resources: so you get the Romans. In the second age, wealth came from inventing and owning manufacturing processes: so you get the Ford Motor Company. Right now all the land that's ever going to be available has already been acquired and demand for manufactured goods is slow, markets are saturated. We all have a microwave, thanks all the same. Double-click here to reveal: the Information Age, whose achievements are measured in dollars and bytes, not empires or production runs. Knowledge is, as they always used to say, power. Only now, more so. Except that we have to use the word 'image' rather than 'knowledge'.

But there's something else immensely significant going on in our millenarian stew. In the Information Age, *appearance* becomes precious while effective symbolism becomes priceless. We may giggle about William Hague's curious aspect, but our sniggers are revealing of a deeper truth about ourselves. Information may be precious – and as rare as substance in politics – but it is intangible, hence style assumes a disproportionate significance. Information has to be packaged. You are what you appear to be, hence poor Mr Hague's problem.

Packaging, of one sort or another, has become one of the great activities of the state. Is it true that Professor Mandelstein has an underground media lab where he practises his image manipulation, his off-the-record briefings and his post-doctoral research into spinning? Whatever, come the Millennium, Britain will be 'rebranded'. There is already some work-in-progress which you can read about on the following pages, an account of People's Britain.

I don't want to be a curmudgeon, but I'm not sure I'm terribly enthused at the prospect of the New Britain as viewed from here. I'm afraid there's no debating the point that totalitarian governments accord special significance to art, architecture and design as expressions of power and authority. There are, for instance, only imperceptible shades of difference between the bloated classical style favoured by Stalin and the bloated classical style favoured by Hitler. Nor is there a world of difference between the Soviet 'party line' and Professor Mandelstein's wince-making neologism 'on message'. Last time we saw a new European government so determined to do things in the name of the People, the word they used was *Volk*. *Volkisch* was the directive and the direction for the Nazi Party's chosen architectural style. If only New Britain had any car manufacturers left, Professor Mandelstein might instruct them to make a People's Car (the ideal vehicle to take for a spin).

Architecture, according to the Romantics, is frozen music. But architecture today has become corporate identity; not so much the mother of the arts as the colleague of the letterhead and the livery. New powers have often sought an expression of their purposes and personality in new, heroic buildings. When Napoleon installed the Wittelsbach family as Kings of Bavaria they promptly set about an ambitious programme of city-building which still defines the character and style of Munich. New money has the same tendency. Nineteenth-century beer and soap barons built themselves castles, as if to acquire via architecture the antique credentials they otherwise lacked. The *parvenu* Rothschilds built a French-style chateau at Waddesdon and a Jacobean-style country house at Ferrières: the theory of exotic validation conferring prestige – or so the theory goes.

Which brings us to the Millennium Dome, the Colosseum or Detroit of Blair's Information Age Empire. It is already the most familiar new building in Britain: a genuine repository for our unease about the present and our hopes for the future. Thus, as a solution which existed before the problem was properly stated, the Millennium Dome perfectly represents a culture where almost everything is sacrificed on the altar of presentation. There is some substance in the tabloid rhetoric: it's an heroic structure which covers a crisis. Yet, so far, the Dome is the most complete symbol of New Britain – which is why it generates such entertaining controversy.

The Millennium Experience is pure *kitsch*, one expression of a philistine government interested in a glib quest for easy solutions dressed in powerful symbolism. Another expression of the same intellectual and artistic deficiencies is a pusillanimous dependence on opinion research and on focus groups. These are not so much the articles of faith of our civilization as its articles of superstition. You cannot impose an architectural solution (on a Millennium or anything else) until you fully understand the problem. Nor should you employ opinion research as a substitute for creative decision-making. But as we will see, in New Britain this is happening all the time.

Maybe the Millennium Dome will eventually accommodate a

successful event: curiosity alone should generate its target traffic, and if curiosity doesn't achieve the visitor targets, a huge advertising budget will. Yet there is something unsettling about this symbol of New Britain. It is this: excellence in design arises from the excellence of an idea. It is as if every interested party from Edison to Conran has said, 95 per cent perspiration and five per cent visualization. It is a matter of thinking. Professor Mandelstein wants it the other way around. This is one reason why the Dome makes people instinctively uneasy: great projects are defined by authenticity and integrity. This is not yet a great project, although it is a very big one. New Britain, People's Britain – or whatever it is currently *styled* – has yet to define the achievements that will give it the symbols worthy of the name.

But it is thrilling that after so many years of neglect, the importance of visual matters is now appreciated by government. Certainly, with or without a capital 'P', people want symbolism. It's just a shame that no one seems to realise that to be effective, symbols must have substance. New Labour's Britain is the essence of Susan Sontag's Camp. She is not the primal source – that can be found in Christopher Isherwood's *The World in the Evening* (1954) – but Sontag's is the most brilliant analysis of a dominant modern sensibility. Sontag explains that 'Camp' is the self-conscious love of the unnatural, a badge of identity for the urbanite. It converts the serious into the frivolous. It is a way of seeing the world in terms only of style. New Labour's Camp puts the style before substance, the symbols before the achievement. 'In matters of great importance' – Sontag now quotes Oscar Wilde in *Lady Windermere's Fan* – 'the vital element is not sincerity, but style.' New Labour is Camp.

Chapter 1

Art Under Dictatorship

'It is not such a huge distance between "party line" and the vile Mandelsonian neologism "off-message".'

Forgive me, I don't myself have access to Excalibur – no software more sinister and manipulative than WordPerfect level 6.0 in my own case – so what follows is mere belief, opinion and surmise. Without all that thrumming technological back-up, I can't be actually certain of what I mean to say. I have to rely on the idea that my world-view is consistent. Maybe, as Nigel Williams mused about himself, it's a world-view forged by a deadly convergence of too much reading and too much bitterness, but I think it's nonetheless (or perhaps I mean *inevitably*) consistent. Consistent is good. Speaking personally, I've never felt the need for mind-control software manufactured and distributed by a member of what flowers-in-their-hair liberals used to call 'the military-industrial conspiracy'. I don't need to check quotes because while I hope I never repeat myself, I always try to say the same thing. Surely that's the same for anyone with integrity? Well, apparently not. Excalibur is the name of the Electronic Filing System software donated to New Labour by the DIY businessman, Philip Jeffrey. It would be melodramatic to call Jeffrey 'secretive', but he does not encourage personal publicity.

Excalibur is simply the most tangible of Clinton's intellectual gifts to New Labour: eager party workers went to Little Rock in 1992 and Washington in 1996 and (not) all they brought back was this lousy software. Back home, they contracted seven young volunteers and paid them well (about £15,000 annually with an additional £1,000 on completion). Their job was to build the information database which the mighty Excalibur would riffle-through in the service of New Labour's aggressive 'instant rebuttal system'.

Running on Sun Microsystems hardware, Excalibur scans 92,000 pages per second. It is an awesome intelligence-gathering tool. Information management software is nothing new, but Excalibur has two features which differentiate it from the ordinary stuff: automatic indexing of the whole content of documents, so you get an image of the text as well as mere copy; and fuzzy-logic search, or APRP (Adaptive Pattern Recognition Processing) which avoids the transcription errors familiar from old-tech Optical Character Recognition systems. It has, as they say in California, got fancy search algorithms dealing with frequency proximity. Since future brain-scanning technologies allow a primitive understanding of what thoughts actually look like, it is only a matter of time before Excalibur or its derivatives can squash dissident thoughts as they emerge . . . long before they get into a troublesome Press.

These toiling party workers were busy scanning in every utterance of Conservative MPs and Ministers, cross-referenced to Reuters' CD-ROMs. Since Excalibur can retrieve not only the actual text, but an image of the original context too, extraordinary feats of rebuttal are now possible. A complacent Conservative MP had simply to mutter an unchecked and unguarded comment on a matter of policy, no matter how minor, and the whirring clicking and clacking electronics of computerized thought-control would confront him with his duplicity: and even its context, to add insult to injury. This was media-monitoring as Star Wars was to the Home Guard. While the Opposition was relying on memory (although Conservative Party HQ had in fact installed Excalibur before New Labour, they clearly had less ability to exploit its advantages), New Labour was martialling billions of instructions-per-second in the cause of the People. Response times were reduced from days to a matter of seconds. A zapping rebuttal was now possible in a single news cycle. Disagreement became very hard work indeed.

Hilariously, although New Labour says it is very keen on a cool, US-style Freedom of Information Act (along with a US-style Drugs Czar, US-style proposals for university fees and US-style 'zero tolerance' measures), it has instructed its client, Excalibur Technologies, not to comment in any way on its application. Labour's own users of Excalibur have to sign non-disclosure documents. While Excalibur was extremely useful in embarrassing dim Tories, it has vast and not yet fully exploited potential for dooming Labour dissidents. Future applications of Excalibur will extend the filing technology to include fingerprints, still and video images, and sound.

The historical Excalibur was Arthur's sword. It is Caledvwlch in the *Mabinogion* and Caladbolg in Irish legend. It seems to mean 'capable of consuming anything' and Excalibur EFS is capable of consuming anything, including facts and opinions. Writing this, I am irresistibly reminded of that marvellous little passage in Burckhardt's *The Civilization of the Renaissance in Italy*. 'It must here be briefly indicated by what steps the art of war assumed the character of a product of reflection.' The martial metaphors are appropriate. The management consultant who helped fix Excalibur for New Labour was John Carr, who was at Little Rock in 1992 where the Clinton team's rebuttal people used the motto 'Speed kills'. Admiration for things American is profound in New Labour, although less is said about a civilization which tolerates (even encourages) a 60-million constituency of the illiterate (according to Paul Fussell in *Bad, or the Dumbing of America*, 1990) than is said about the media manipulation techniques which create Presidential stars in either country.

The chilling and incontrovertible authority of Excalibur is in nice contrast to the altogether less precise phenomenon which dominates the People's Britain as defined by New Labour. We see more style to this government than we hear about substance. We are in the world of the pseudo-event, defined by the Librarian of Congress, Daniel Boorstin, in his great book *The Image: or What Happened to the American Dream* (1962) as something:

1   not spontaneous, but planned;
2   whose purpose is to generate press coverage;
3   which does not distinguish between fact and fiction, truth and reality, but whose distinguishing characteristic is newsworthiness;
4   which, while it has an ambiguous relationship to 'reality', tends to be self-fulfilling.

Pseudo-events are not so much unreal as artificial. Thus a Press Release marked 'For Future Release' *becomes* news, whatever its merits. Thus, rock stars at Downing Street become news. That pseudo-events are so influential in public life is an inevitable consequence of a civilization and a government obsessed with the media. It was in the 1960s that the vast appetite of the media, the need to fill a news-stream that was moving ever faster, created a demand for the pseudo-event, although the founding fathers of PR had predicted their coming forty years earlier, as readers of Walter Lippmann's *Public Opinion* (1922) will know. Pseudo-events are complementary to the arcane but well-publicized practice of spin doctoring. Each treats news as something to be invented and managed, not reported and analysed. Nowadays, when a politician speaks off the cuff, it causes alarm and surprise. There has been no opportunity for spin! It may be a real event, not an imagined one! What is scary about pseudo-events is that they question the philosophical basis of 'reality'.

The first politician to develop the skills which later evolved into the pseudo-event and into spin was Joseph R. McCarthy, the senator for Wisconsin in the decade following 1947. McCarthy was, of course, also known for his own strong views about dissidents. His was the primal pseudo-event: the press conference to announce a future press conference. As soon as it was discovered as a potent political weapon, this appetite for fake information was further stimulated by exponential growth in communications technology. It was a century from the dryplate camera to the VCR, but in fifteen years we have added global round-the-clock media, satellite and cable TV, minicams, PCs, e-mail, Internet, mobile phones, faxes and ISDN. If pseudo-events were a happy chance discovery of unscrupulous politicians, then an unimaginable proliferation of news media kept supply and demand in athletic relationship.
What concerns me most seriously about the style of New Labour is not simply the appetite for pseudo-events, but something in the actual structure of its world-view which is reminiscent of the most sinister period of recent European history. Here is a government which strikes liberal poses, but is

in fact decidedly authoritarian. Without wanting to indulge in hysterical exaggeration, New Labour's obsession with style and propaganda has much in common – at least in the structural sense recognised by anthropologists and historians – with the fascist governments of pre-war Germany and Italy.

In his magisterial study of this subject, *Art Under Dictatorship* (1954), Hellmut Lehmann-Haupt wrote:

> **'I never cease to wonder . . . how powerful ideas can be which have very little, if any, foundation in truth; how the fact that concepts do not logically hang together does not seem to prevent them from materializing into very hard and solid reality.'**

In New Britain, rock stars assemble at Downing Street to advertise the government's coolness. At one level this is just tacky, but at another level it is frightening. There are other aspects of New Britain which force telling comparisons with older authoritarian governments:

- The need for symbolism (*viz.* Dome)
- Reliance on bogus research (*viz.* focus groups)
- Distrust of experts (*viz.* experts – may be elitist)
- Celebrity cults (*viz.* rock stars at Number 10)
- A public taste for sentimentality, ready to be exploited by cynical politicians (*viz.* too-hasty manipulation of Diana cult)

The Nazis and Soviets used rigid censorship and highly persuasive propaganda. They exploited sentiment. The dictators of each country, at least presentationally speaking, attached a central role to the arts (although experimentation and dissent were not so much discouraged as ruthlessly crushed). It is, I think, not such a huge distance between 'party line' and the vile Mandelsonian neologism 'off message'. And they invoke 'People'.

Dictatorships develop very strong views about art, since even bad art has the power to rouse 'People'. Dictators cannot tolerate art that penetrates the surface of the world, nor any art that is apprehensive or even negative. Dictators do not want art that contains elements of prophecy (that could get confused too easily with their own propaganda). The dictator requires that art should be easy to 'read', unproblematic and unchallenging. This is very much the 'message' of the Department of Culture, Media and Sport. The Dictator must both please and dominate through the arts. You would need a dissertation to examine the precise links between Arno Breker (a realist sculptor favoured by the Nazis) and Elton John, but I'm certain there's something in it.

However, it's important to recognize an irony here. While authoritarian governments are deeply distrustful of experimental art, it must be conceded by even the most fanatical experimentalist that 'political' art never changed a thing. Picasso's *Guernica* has imaginative power, dignity, profound psychology and novel form, in that it is most certainly an authentic work of art; and, of course, its influence on the Franco regime was in real terms non-existent. Only the media can influence thought – which is why, in People's Britain, the only art that has official approval is the sort that can acquire leveraged significance because it is reported on the telly. Hence, the Turner Prize: evidence of an art world which, in Robert Hughes' words, is 'trivialized by money and fashion [and] can't tell a Leonardo from a scribble' (*The Culture of Complaint,* 1993).

The idea of a People's Britain suggests that those People have little knowledge of history. It is sinister. Dictators talk about the 'People' because it is a cynical shortcut to establishing the sense of uncritical national purpose needed to sustain their power. But Daniel Boorstin insisted that any idea of national purpose is 'largely an illusion', adding rather sorrowfully that it was also 'one of the most popular illusions of our time'. He believed that the real problems in the contemporary world were personal, not collective. Yet here we find Chris Smith, Secretary of State for Culture, Media and Sport and the author of a widely ridiculed book called *Creative Britain* suggesting that the great thing about Diana was that the events following her death suggested 'a real feeling that we are coming together as a nation, in shared grief but in shared purpose too'. If Smith had read Hellmut Lehmann-Haupt and Daniel Boorstin he would not be able to write such utter rubbish. The sinister character of the Diana cult went entirely undetected by the Pooterish Smith with his Orwellian title. The cult was, as Roger Kimball has pointed out, a 'counterfeit emotion'. The problem with counterfeit emotions is that they are susceptible to manipulation and direction by dictators.

At the same time, a belief in a 'People' (rather like the belief in the existence of the 'society' which Mrs Thatcher denied in a coloratura burst of libertarianism) suggests that the individual should subsume himself in communal purpose. Does this sound familiar, voters? Labour Camp cannot tolerate individual dissent. Hence, Excalibur. Hence the glorification of collective aims in the Branding of Britain.

In a revealing diary entry for 17th September 1997, Lord Runciman noted some characteristic comings and goings at No. 10:

> **'As I sit quietly in the entrance hall . . . Next appears Robin Cook, who is led aside by Alastair Campbell and rehearsed in conspiratorial whispers about what he is to say to the reptiles waiting across the road. Cook, whom I've never met, gives me a quick, suspicious look. Alastair, whom I have, carefully ignores me. The Supremo of Spin moves over to the window, looks across, signals; the front door is again opened, the Foreign Secretary emerges on cue, the cameras flash, the door closes behind him. I reflect that it's more like a stage set than a stage set.'**

It makes you wonder what exactly is Tony Blair's conception of the British *Volk*, the People whose authority he invokes at every opportunity. What is the stage we are acting upon? Certainly, the play we are acting out on it is full of absurd contradictions and alarming warnings. At the funeral of Diana on 6th September 1997, popular feeling was given precedence over rank, tradition and history even though, as Anthony O'Hear explained, 'without rank, tradition and history there would be no Di'. The intellectual basis for the elevation of the People is feeble where it is not disturbing.

Eric Bettelheim is the son of Dachau survivor and influential child psychologist Bruno Bettelheim. From his unique perspective, a Knightsbridge-based American derivatives lawyer with access to an unusual cultural inheritance which mixes rabbinical discipline with the intellectual vigour of the University of Chicago, Bettelheim says he finds that modern Britons tend to act like a 'medieval hysterical mob'. So far from finding the Diana phenomenon a moving testament to national grief, he detected an undertow of repressed unarticulated violence.

The Diana phenomenon is significant if you want to understand a culture where lasting values are sacrificed to presentation: 'Oprah Winfrey writ large' as Bettelheim puts it. It was a defining moment. This is why there was such a ferocious response to Professor Anthony O'Hear's account of the Diana cult in a controversial anthology, Faking It (1998). Anyone who has actually read Professor O'Hear's essay knows that it is in fact a sober, unhysterical and well-judged piece of academic popularisation. O'Hear says Diana stood for 'the elevation of feeling, image and spontaneity over reason, reality and restraint'. To illustrate the point he explains that in 'New Britain . . . the mother of the future king publicly weeps at the funeral of a vulgar and self-publicizing Italian dress designer'. And, entirely appropriately, the Princess of Wales shared her tears on this occasion with the lachrymose Elton John.

Bettelheim says:

> **'Blair's spontaneous reaction to Faking It made it crystal clear he hadn't actually read it. His spontaneous response was to defend a popular cause.**

What Blair had detected in the Diana phenomenon was a huge media opportunity, bigger even than one of Professor Mandelstein's pseudo-events. The crowds in Kensington Gardens were like a non-stop vast free and informal focus group, a volatile and potent mixture of popular culture and what O'Hear calls 'undogmatic religiosity'. Maybe the emotions of the crowd were genuine: that is not even the point. The point is, as Eric Bettelheim explained, a government which takes advantage of crude populism and even seeks to stimulate it is the 'beginning of dictatorship'.

More so than Daniel Boorstin might ever have realized, government is now in the hands of image-builders and those who know how to exploit imagery. Under dictatorships, the art best practised is the one of self-deception. As Lehmann-Haupt knew, dictatorships always fail, not just in moral terms, but in artistic ones too. There is always a vast discrepancy between intention and result, between purpose and achievement. That's why I think that, under this mildest and most amiable of dictatorships, we are all witnessing the failure of style over substance.

Chapter 2

Branding Britain

'T. S. Eliot said that "culture" ("national identity" had not yet been invented) was everything from Early English cathedrals to boiled cabbage. He didn't know the half of it.'

Patriotism is, of course, the last refuge of the scoundrel, and novelty is the same destination for the adman with no good ideas. In their ceaseless quest for public approval, officials have not yet offered free sex, but a vision of a 'New' Britain is up for appraisal. When I read that the sleepy, enervated old Design Council (founded in 1936 as an uncharacteristically stylish flourish of the Imperial Board of Trade) had commissioned the very switched-on Demos (a policy inventor so bright, so pulsing with the throb of the 200w Zeitgeist that it is plugged directly into the Downing Street grid) to write a report about the 'branding of Britain', a little fantasy began to develop in my mind.

It was a slow afternoon at the new Department of Corporate Identity. Although the civil servants had willingly voted to move from stuffy Whitehall to a site between Oddbins and Gap in Islington's Upper Street, many of the old guard regretted the change. It was all very well for the Secretary of State for Brand Values to argue that it was essential to be conveniently situated for all the restaurants favoured by the Department's high-profile image consultant, Wally Pantone, but it just didn't feel like real government in N1. Besides, the more traditional members of staff were embarrassed by the compulsory Burberry-patterned baseball caps which carried Wally Pantone's new British identity logo, a stylized tranche of seared polenta with a sprig of roast rosmarino and a little pyramid of sun-dried tomatoes above the cringe-making strapline 'Warm beer and cricket: Out! Out! Out!' Then suddenly, anticipated by intoxicating vapours of Floris lavender scent, the Junior Minister for Emblematic Constructs rushed in, waving sit-reps, mission statements, opinion research, data capture and a Paul Smith nuova-Britmode *bandana. 'Bugger!' he screamed, 'I've just had a meeting at Granita with Wally Pantone, David Puttnam and the Minister for Cognitive Dissonance. They've insisted on putting the new Welsh flag out to a focus group. 75 per cent of A1, B1s in Carmarthen won't accept the coypu as a mascot and there's a feeling we should reinstate the dragon, leek and daffodil. And this is just ten days before the Prime Minister has to relaunch Dyfed as The Geoffrey of Monmouth Centre$^{\circledR}$ and Simply Red's remix of the Mabinogion is released.'*

And then when I actually read the little book, *Britain™: Renewing Our Identity* the fantasy evaporated and I wanted to pick it up and throw it across the room. This arose from the Design Council's initiative on 'A New Brand for Britain', sent to Downing Street on election day, 1997. Rarely have I read such a specious, fatuous collection of half-truths. Sorry, let me correct that: dated half-truths. The author was Mark Leonard, a Demos intern and son of veteran Fabian writer and political consultant, Dick Leonard. Young Leonard argues well (in the same way that those people irritatingly good at debates used to at school), but both his prose style and personal presentation lack flair. The folly of having an influential report about national identity, a matter of aesthetics, written by someone with no apparent interest in the visual, is a depressingly apt emblem of New Britain where an obsession with appearances does not entail any very precise aesthetic awareness.

Science provides marvellous metaphors of human frailty and foibles. Who does not know a sluggish individual whose intellectual limitations are not best described by saying he has

Read-Only Memory (ROM)? How many once promising, but fatally stalled, careers can be described by that chilling abbreviation from aerospace, CFIT or Controlled Flight Into Terrain, the accident investigator's emotionally neutral expression for a crash that occurs when the flight crew is apparently fully alert and functioning.

But best of all is that expression from particle physics which provides a metaphor of all the spiritual conundrums, paradoxes and ironies of the modern world (not to mention the tortured question of national identity): the uncertainty principle. This was the great theoretical physicist Werner Heisenberg's term for that perverse phenomenon which occurs when you attempt to investigate the precise behaviour of capricious and spritely subatomic matter. The very act of investigation alters the behaviour the investigator is seeking to understand. Merely thinking about neutrinos makes them stamp their feet and shout 'Shan't! Won't.' Nothing is certain.

Thus, the absurdity of rebranding Britain. The vexatious matter of national identity is a delicate and precarious mixture of shared symbols, happy accidents, evolutionary chaos, historical inheritance, genetic roulette, political interference, history of artistic whim, palaeo-anthropology, economics, the weather, geology, sunspots, Iron Age migration patterns, religion, bus routes, taste, sex, the Gulf Stream, football results and investment decisions made in Lower Saxony and Detroit.

The essence of nationhood and its visual expression is an unknowably complicated and subtle amalgam of fact, fiction and prejudice. T. S. Eliot said that 'culture' ('national identity' had not yet been invented) was everything from Early English cathedrals to boiled cabbage. He didn't know the half of it. National identity is easier to detect than define, still less direct. At one level, it is a matter of serious scholarly speculation. A collection of essays edited by Brendan Bradshaw and Peter Roberts, *British Consciousness and Identity – The Making of Britain 1533–1707* (1998) is typical of this academic genre. The French say that we are *cent ans de retard et dix ans d'avance*. That summarizes the oddity of the subject rather nicely.

The elements of our national identity are pleasingly contradictory. We have a brilliant reputation as technical innovators and a lamentable one as production engineers. The idiosyncratic genius of finding solutions to problems that don't exist (the hovercraft is a paradigm here) is a sacred attribute of nationhood. And so is the extraordinary skill of doing unlikely things unusually well – British India is an example. Never has an entire civilization been better characterized than saying the British are an illustration of that old principle: the people who start businesses shouldn't run them.

We maintain in fastidious order some of Europe's oldest and most unworldly and irrelevant institutions, but at the same time cultivate the most energetic and irreverent and disrespectful and innovative youth culture. We support world-class research and development in truly difficult things like medicine, civil engineering, avionics and pharmaceuticals, but do not possess the means to manufacture a simple five-ton panel van without foreign investment. The nation that invented the television cannot make one. Despite a reputation for being resolute philistines, we excel in all creative activities, from advertising to architecture through theatre, music, art and design.

These curious bi-attitudes are all part of our national identity, but, as the uncertainty principle dictates, as soon as you develop a sense of self-consciousness about so delicate, subtle and complex a network of ideas and beliefs, you distort it. If you try to interfere with national identity, it disappears. Of course, you can photograph it, but the photographic image is momentary, dead, stationary, fixed and arbitrary: national identity is more like smoke and sunbeams.

But in an age when brand values are the chief point of difference between manufactured goods, there is a well-argued, if ill-considered, argument for creating a 'brand for Britain'. Coming from the world of Flora, Tampax, Hobnobs and Doritos, a brand is that numinous quantity which accountants in simpler, more innocent days, used to call 'goodwill'. A brand is goodwill with a trademark attached. Except that when we speak of trademarks we have to call them logos, a logo being a trademark that went to art school and lives in Soho or Covent Garden.

Anybody who really wants to, can make a carbonated beverage with herbal extracts; but only one company can make Coca-Cola, a brand whose success is at least as much associated with its rich iconography (sustained by a $3.8 billion annual marketing budget) as it is with its 'delicious and refreshing' taste. The argument goes that to be modern and successful like Diet Coke, Diet Britain needs a brand. This argument ignores the self-evident truth that, while delicious and refreshing, Coke is an elemental product with one dimension and one taste. Great Britain is not. It is more complicated. And if we would all welcome some distance from the quaint Ye Olde Ogilvy & Mather visual clichés which dominated the tourist perception of Britain since the 1950s, the coruscating alternative – of national destiny being in the hands of spoon-faced trainee brand managers who think 1688 is a French lager – is not welcome either.

Comparisons with industry do not offer much comfort to the men from the Ministry of Emblematic Constructs. While it is inevitable that at a time when information is the chief commodity of economic exchange and the intangibles of the 'brand' become paramount, at the same time it is indisputable that in the commercial world the most successful brands are those that have evolved through history and nurture, not the ones that were produced at a 'brainstorm' after lunch at The Groucho Club.

Coca-Cola, Ford, Mercedes-Benz and Sony are exemplars. Coke uses the copperplate signature of its original. The Ford story is similar. Sony was a glorious Japanese misunderstanding of phonetic English ('sonic') mixed with a valuable insight that two syllables were easier on Western ears than Tokyo Tsushin Kogyo Kabushika Kaika, combined with an abuse of the classic Clarendon typeface. Mercedes-Benz will never, ever change its three-pointed star. Those more recently invented brands are a sorry bunch of neophytes.

Whenever entire countries have attempted to invent or reinvent national identity, the results have tended to be sinister. The most compelling and thoroughgoing identity scheme of all was the one prepared on behalf of the Volk by the National Sozialister Deutsche Arbeiter Partei and so eagerly adopted by the Luftwaffe, Wehrmacht, Gestapo, Schutzstaffel and Kriegsmarine. The Red Army was pretty sassy too, but hindered by a comparative lack of creative resources.

And equally, the countries with the strongest identities are those that are least self-conscious about it: the mere suggestion of red, white and green suggests both tomato, mozarella and basil as well as the Italian tricolore – and that's really all that needs to be said about it. Wally Pantone would have charged a few hundred thousand to attain this universal perception. No developed nation is less fussed than Italy about the maintenance of its past or present image: none has a stronger identity.

The Demos arguments in favour of renewing national identity are not all wrong: many are the familiar stuff of discourse among architects and designers, and have been for years. For instance, of course it would be a good idea if the major arrival and departure points for rail, air and sea were more attractive, better designed. The traveller's first and last encounters with British institutions are often depressing. This side of a Romanian psychiatric institution, Heathrow Airport is one of the nastiest places on earth. While it is absolutely clear what everyone wants from an airport, namely calm, clarity, quiet, comfort and an atmosphere of elegant and confident expectation appropriate to the great technological adventure of flight, what BAA plc provides is altogether different. It provides garish and clamorous factory outlets over a large and wretchedly congested and cluttered part of Middlesex. BAA plc does not see its responsibilities as being the stewardship of passengers, but as a profit funnel for shareholders. Accordingly, while there is no public space worthy of the name in the vast barbarian sprawl of Heathrow, the harassed traveller is instead given every opportunity to buy single malt whisky, cashmere socks, caviar, a Chinese camera and a dress shirt.

Yes, the deplorable state of Heathrow and Euston and Paddington and Dover and Holyhead is a big architectural and design problem which we'd be grateful if the relevant authorities remedied. That's a straightforward matter of taste and style and what the art historians used to call *Kunstwollen*: the simple desire to make something artistic. But other parts of the Demos strategy for New Britain are less well considered and less well argued. At its worst, Britain™ reads like a transcript of an early Thatcher-period dinner party in Highgate where the guests included not only Wally Pantone, but his neighbour, the advertising guru Bart Bogle-Hegarty, the image consultant Peter Yorkie-Barr and Professor Michael Porter, visiting from Harvard Business School and working, at the time, on his toe-breaking hypnotic, *The Competitive Advantage of Nations* (1990).

Thus the bulk of Britain™ is familiar, tired and inappropriate, betraying lots of unexamined borrowings, not least the irritatingly cute ™, a revealing Americanism, like so much else in the People's newly rebranded Britain. These people are in doe-like thrall to everything Stateside, from Clinton's largesse to Excalibur's information management. But their data is not uptodate. The citation of the troubled German white goods manufacturer, AEG, as an exemplary case study in the management of corporate identity, while it has some historical credentials, does not inspire confidence that the author knows what he is talking about. AEG, created by the cosmopolitan entrepreneurs Emil and Walter Rathenau, was once a worthy pioneer in the German electrical industry, but since its heavy-handed takeover by Daimler-Benz has become a demoralized element of an ungainly conglomerate. Another exhausted anecdote refers to Dixons, the garish retailer. Demos is desperately agitated that Dixons calls its own-brand consumer products by a bogus Japanese name, Matsui. Never mind that the majority of these Matsui products are sourced from Asia, it would not make sense to call an electronic consumer product by anything other than a Japanese name. They have the credentials, the culture and the image capital. No-one would want a video cassette recorder called a Parker-Bowles 1066AD.

These are just two examples of muddle-headed and ploddingly literal thinking about the fugitive nature of national identity. But worse than the bungled argument and the lazy citation of irrelevant and dated facts larded with half-baked rabble-rousing opinion is the pervasive aroma of something so antiquated that it's decomposing: corporatism. Hands up anyone who remembers Anthony Wedgwood-Benn (whose own pioneering rebranding exercise turned himself into a pre-Blair Tony) and his MinTech of the 1960s. MinTech was a chromium-plated, one-hundred-per-cent, hands-on, utterly committed disaster for

British technology, stimulating the steady and undramatic descent of the native motor industry into a catastrophic deep stall from which it never recovered. At the same time as cancelling innovative military aerospace programmes, it committed the civil aviation business to ruinous participation with the United States, effectively excluding British airframe and engine contractors from the dominant role they deserved in the first twenty years of the successful European Airbus project.

Demos did not create MinTech, but there is a shared taste for corporatist stratagems. It is a pity that our desire to learn from the American example is only partial. No sooner had Mobil decided, circa 1966, that in the interests of global reach and good design management every single filling-station on the planet should be made to look exactly the same, than someone else discovered that maybe New Zealand had local requirements for its forecourts which were different from those which dominated the market in northern Sweden.

There have been very, very few successful world brands and, so far, no examples whatsoever of a successfully contrived national identity. Doubters may wish to inspect the melancholy ruins of Mussolini's ideal towns of Latina and Sabaudia to confirm this opinion. Heathrow may be an ugly and chaotic zoo, but it is a free and vigorous one which, talking about idiosyncratic genius, actually works rather well. I'm not certain that anyone would prefer it if the Secretary of State for Brand Values had called in his Ministers for Emblematic Constructs and Cognitive Dissonance and had convened focus groups and opinion polls, and drawn up guidelines for rebranding Britain.

The muddled Demos report was commissioned by the Design Council under the chairmanship of John Sorrell, a crafty professional designer whose own second-generation (third, if you count Lippincott & Margulies in Chicago in the 1950s) business, Newell and Sorrell, was recently sold to Interbrand plc, the consultancy that has given the world the Hobnob biscuit. Under Sorrell the Design Council has reinvented itself, going long on flashy graphics, but remaining very short indeed on serious research or intellectually respectable methodology. Issues of identity greatly concern Sorrell, whose recent overhaul of British Airways has not been well received either inside or outside the airline. Inside, things are so bad that its implementation has been slowed and Phase II is known as 'the recovery programme'. Outside, it is considered a gaudy emblem of Bob Ayling's troubled regime; so much so that it has been routinely cited as a cause in scurrilous newspaper stories hinting at Ayling's termination.

The 'new' British Airways corporate is a perfect example of how misleading technical research into the intuitive area of identity can be. This research indicated that the majority of British Airways flights originated outside the UK, a trend that will increase as this global carrier takes advantage of increasing deregulation of the airline business and seeks strategic alliances with American Airlines, among others. In the icy logic of research, the figures show that sixty per cent of passengers are not British nationals, still less that they feel any bond with the British Isles. The argument therefore developed that, since British Airways is a global 'brand' (steadily divesting itself of useful, but expensive, material resources: engineering, for instance), there is no good reason to have the Union flag, or a version of it, on the tailfin of the company's aircraft (a motif put there by San Francisco design company Landor Associates, among much controversy, in 1983). Never mind that the sight of a BA tailfin has lifted many disconsolate spirits at crabby airports around the planet, the remorseless *reductio ad absurdum* of this perception would, of course, be to drop the 'British' bit altogether.

They did not get that far, but they did get pretty absurd. Sorrell's team interpreted this research in an ingenious manner. Invigorated by the prospect of one of the biggest corporate identity jobs of all, they decided to express the globalized, politically correct vigour and unaligned cosmopolitanism of the airline with folk art. So, from around the world they started on a remarkable programme of commissioning and collecting vernacular art expressive of the hundreds of destinations served by BA's fleet. A Delft tile here, a Zulu shield or aboriginal bark painting there. Never mind that these colourful devices and conceits rarely fitted the trapezoid fins of Boeings, the solution was accepted as a corporate identity 'that is more than a mere style, rather a communications solution with a literally inexhaustible range of applications. If British Airways has become a brand of world travel, it's not too fanciful to imagine this new identity one day appearing on more than fins and fuselages'. Or so it was thought. The opposing view was that a dignified and well-known identity which had accumulated considerable respect over the years by consistent application and its association with good service was now dissipated in an unco-ordinated jumble of meaningless primitivism and a token sort of globalism comprehensible only to an interbred claque of marketing and design cronies.

The problem was, while the Newell & Sorrell rebranding of
British Airways was exciting and unconventional and ignored
the orthodoxies, no one had the common sense to realize that
passengers, whatever passport they hold or from wheresoever
they 'originate', do not want airlines to be exciting,
unconventional and unorthodox. At 35,000 feet, most people
crave reassurance with the familiar. Never in all consumer
experience have there been stronger arguments for a service
provider being deeply, deeply conservative and orthodox. You
want your airline to be run by a bridge-playing golfer married to
a Conservative councillor who drives a prestige estate car and
has three children at good public schools. Newell & Sorrell has
given the impression that British Airways, with its inappropriate
primitive art, is run by Stone-Age nomads.

Undeterred by the creation of a 'new' British Airways that was
less popular than its predecessor, Sorrell, now back in his
Design Council role, was also responsible for the 1997 Annual
Report, more evidence of second-rate thinking and the insistent
desire to put style in front of substance. The Report contains no
hint of a sensible operating definition of 'design'. The dodgy
methodology is made more annoying by untested assumptions
and claims. The design of the Report (whose contents would,
on intellectual and commercial grounds, justify no more than
two pages), is fussy, wasteful and positively clamours for
attention with a bad-mannered noisiness. The clichés rain like
friendly bombs on Slough: things are 'up and running', a 'leap
forward' is anticipated and in the favourite trope of modernizers

everywhere there is to be a 'sea change' of something or other.
The Millennium Products project (launched by Blair in
September 1997, absorbing 33 per cent of the annual £7.05
million budget) will identify 2,000 'icons' by the turn of the
century. This, a warmed-up version of the old Design Council
awards, had – the last time I looked – not a chance of notching
up many more than ten meaningful innovations. And to get to
even that number you have to include a shoe for cows and a
duvet cover that conveniently opens on three sides.

Under New Labour, the Department of Trade and Industry
birthed Powerhouse:uk, a landmark of vintage 1998 Labour
Camp, something to do with 'putting the UK's future image
under the spotlight'. Note that cool image thing. In an
incongruous wheezing inflatable in William Kent's stately
Horseguards, a somewhat familiar selection of British industrial
and commercial achievements was presented for the stimulus
of visiting politicians. The egregious Dyson cleaner, chief
industrial icon of New Britain, was naturally included. Jacques
Derrida and Roland Barthes should have encountered the
Dyson. Deconstructing its symbolic value for New Britain would
have entertained the Café Flore seminar for the best part of an
afternoon. Many Dysons are in fact manufactured in France.
Conventional German machines perform better. James Dyson is
an inventor of great talent and a self-promoter of cosmic genius.
The machines which carry his name are intrusive and demand
attention, but soon irritate. Like New Labour's New Britain, the
Dyson is a bit of a travesty, and Powerhouse:uk was a bit of an
embarrassment.

The Design Council is not always light on its feet. The Annual Report announces with a revelatory air that 'The signs are that design is making an impact beyond industry too.' I must remember that next time I buy something: it really is an amazingly fresh perception. 'Branding Britain' is a misconceived notion. Even advertising professionals, who might be expected to salivate at the profitable aspects of the concept, are dubious because the idea of branding such a complex entity as a nation implies a degree of control which no one possesses. Besides, which brand manager would feel Trainspotting presented an attractive image to prospective foreign investors in youth?

'The campaign to rebrand Britain' wrote Roger Kimball, managing editor of New Criterion, 'requires that the country's past be held as perpetual hostage to the propaganda commitments of the moment' (newspaper report, 30th June 1998). As an authority on Elizabethan court ritual, Sir Roy Strong, Fellow of the Society of Antiquaries, knows a bit about the historical basis of Britain's brand values and its dependence on continuity. I asked him what he thought Powerhouse:uk contributed to a tradition that included Inigo Jones and Purcell. He had a simple answer. He said it was 'Utterly naff, crap, junk.' I imagine he thinks the same about Demos' plans to renew Britain's identity.

Chapter 3

Cool Britannia

'To find a contemporary government, let
alone a contemporary government that
styles itself as "New", showing such a
witless interst in the most gormless forms
of neophilia is embarrassing.'

What more compelling symbol of transformation can there *ever* have been than the one which changed Reginald Kenneth Dwight (b. 1947) into Elton Hercules John (b. 1967)? Here was inspiration of an extremely high order. It predicts and reflects with hypnotic accuracy the transformation of old Labour (b. 27th February, 1900) into the sleek, heroic New version (b. 1992) where Reg and Ken are not welcome, need not apply. And to support the metaphor, each transformation has its supporting characteristics of shiny, brittle, petulant vanity to replace the more homely (but 'old') traits of its predecessor. The rich semantic dissonance between Reg and Hercules has an authentic, unforced hilarity that transcends mocking comment.

It is not surprising that rock music has been appropriated as the chief expression of the People's Art in the Magic Kingdom of Cool Britannia. A radical 'New' government finds it incredibly, sloppily convenient to bypass the tiresome and time-consuming business of earning respect and building up credentials by enlisting council household names to represent New Britain. But even in this fact-free Wonderland, the preferment under New Labour of Elton John has been astonishing. In *Faking It* (1998) Anthony O'Hear made the memorable observation that to have Elton John playing at the funeral of Diana was as absurd as having Vera Lynn singing at the funeral of George VI. But in New Labour's Magic Kingdom it actually happened.

But this one-time rocker turned plaintive balladeer has become the chief sentimentalist of the New Labour regime, although I must concede that, these days at least, cool he is not. But knighted he is. We cannot say whether this honour was designed so as to divert the passions of the Diana cult into votes for New Labour or to acknowledge services to export. The art may be dodgy, but the record is awesome: a generation of low-to-middle brows has grown up to 'Your Song' (1971), 'Rocket Man' (1972), 'Crocodile Rock' (1972), 'Daniel' (1973), 'Candle in the Wind' (1974), 'Don't Go Breaking My Heart' (1976). Elton John is suburbia amplified: he is to the True Story of Rock what Barry Norman is to *Cahiers du Cinema*. His Diana Dirge is the best-selling record of all time, easily out-sentimentalizing *White Christmas*.

He is a popular phenomenon, therefore it is irrelevant and elitist even to wonder if he is actually any good. He is emphatically middle-of-the-road. He is classless. After a much-reported past of rock-star excess, he is clean, dried out. His career was just about ready for a valedictory 'Yet More Greatest Hits' when fate intervened and he relaunched himself. Whoever would have thought you could relaunch old Labour? Whoever would have thought you could relaunch Elton John? The parallels between the two transformations are remarkable.

Late May 1998, Elton performed at Stormont in Northern Ireland. It was, from all reports, immensely moving, a clear recognition of what can be achieved when popular culture works in the cause of Cool Britannia. It was, according to Mo Mowlam, the Northern Ireland Secretary, a 'truly historic occasion'. She went on to praise Sir Elton for his consistent dedication to the Irish (to coin a truly memorable phrase) 'in good times and bad'.The composer of 'Crocodile Rock' emphatically did not shed crocodile tears. He had been clasped to the bosom of Ulster. And what, a *Times* reporter asked the Secretary of State, is your very favourite Elton John song? She didn't know. Couldn't answer. Had a memory lapse. Perhaps couldn't care.

Curiously, although archaeologists of jargon are not exactly agreed on this, 'Cool Britannia' seems to have been a re-invention (or, at least, an opportunistic re-discovery) of Virginia Bottomley's regime at the Department of National Heritage. Cool Britannia has become a hot issue, as quickly disavowed by embarrassed ministers as it was earlier accepted with credulous enthusiasm. Cool Britannia was the inevitable (although, it seems, temporary) destination of a journey that began with the branding of Britain.

If you ask me, there's a big problem with the idea of 'cool'. First, it's a period label so antiquated that its only effective use is an *ironical* one. No-one over twenty in their right mind ever actually refers to anything as 'cool', other than ironically. The origins of the term are instructive. From the well-worn usage 'as cool as a cucumber', meaning unflustered and composed, there was an easy (if surreal) conceptual leap to describe the stoned and groovy composure of jazz musicians Charlie Parker and Miles Davis (whose 'The Birth of Cool' was recorded in 1949–50). That locates the idea at somewhat of a distance in time. And in space. We are talking of New York in the 1950s. 'Cool' is a quaint archaism.

To find a contemporary government, let alone a contemporary government that styles itself as 'New', showing such a witless interest in the most gormless forms of neophilia is embarrassing. Of course, the actual expression 'Cool Britannia' has its own origins in the 1960s (when it was ironically employed most notably by Viv Stanshall of the Bonzo Dog Band). To be momentarily fair, the term has never been officially endorsed by the government, but on the other hand, discounting current hasty disavowals, never has it been energetically rejected. In that it's a lazy cliché which evokes a rather dopey concept of style, it is characteristic of a Camp regime which insists on appearance over substance.

Cool Britannia mugged the intellectuals. After so many years of positive anti-aesthetics – if she thought about art at all, one imagines Mrs Thatcher thought it wet – a government which said it was interested in style appeared to be a very good thing. To appropriate an expression of Mrs Thatcher's, architects and designers and film-makers and artists thought that they could do business in a New Britain whose government did not repudiate art, but positively wallowed in it. But the quality of that wallowing, like the intellectual depths in which it took place, proved irredeemably shallow. In the breathless rush to have all symbols of modernization in place and shining very brightly, the Prime Minister has provided eloquent and damaging evidence of superficiality. He does this at media tie-in parties at Downing Street where the guest list looks like what Sir Roy Strong scornfully described as 'sweepings'. Much, much easier to be seen and, more importantly, to be photographed hugging Mick Hucknall of Simply Red than to radicalize intellectual property law or reinvent music on the National Curriculum.

Here the problem changes again. I don't, I'm glad to say, know what Mick Hucknall thinks, but I don't want rock stars – even middle-of-the-road housewives'-choice, first-time caller, greatest-hits, in-car CD-player rock stars – enrolled as the consorts of politicians. The relationship is doubly damaging, coarsening one party and neutralizing the other. As Picasso knew, authentic art is always seditious. Explaining the invention of Cubism, he said 'We didn't any longer want to fool the eye, we wanted to fool the mind.' And later elaborated 'The point is, art is something subversive. It's something that should *not* be free. Art and liberty, like the fire of Prometheus, are things one must steal, to be used against the established order. Once art becomes official and open to everyone, then it becomes the new academicism. . . If art is ever given the keys to the city, it will be because it's been so watered down, rendered so impotent, that it's not worth fighting for . . . Every poet and every artist is an anti-social being. He's not that way because he wants to be; he can't be any other way. Of *course* the state has the right to chase him away – from *its* point of view – and if he is really an artist it is in his nature not to want to be admitted, because if he is admitted it can only mean he is doing something which is understood, approved and therefore old hat – worthless.' The paradox: governments do not like subversion.

The pursuit of coolness, either explicit or unacknowledged, is a self-denying ordinance. It is just like the nightmare individual who comes up to you at a party and says 'I have been told I have an exceptionally interesting personality.' There is nothing so depressingly ordinary as the desire to appear exceptional. As G. K. Chesterton once remarked, 'All men are ordinary men; the extraordinary men are those that know it.' Wanting to be cool immediately and irrevocably disqualifies you from ever being so. Miles Davis did not need this explaining to him. So far from being cool, the new government's position is timorous and unprincipled. It is sweaty and tacky.

Even if it were an intelligent and attractive policy (itself a prospect requiring a nationwide suspension of disbelief), a notion as crude as Cool Britannia is pitiably thin and one-dimensional. William James gave readers of *The Principles of Psychology*, 1890, an interesting definition of 'self':

> **'The sum total of all that [an individual] can call his, not only his body and his psychic power, but his clothes, and his house, his wife and children, his ancestors and friends, his reputation and works, his lands and horses and yacht and bank account.'**

Which is to say that William James knew that anybody's self, notwithstanding the relative rarity of the horses and the yachts, is complex, various and eclectic. And rather as Picasso insisted that creativity cannot be managed or directed, so a national identity, still less a self-consciously cynical and self-promoting cool national identity, cannot be managed or imposed. As soon as you become self-conscious about any aspect of national identity, it becomes an onerous embarrassment.

Significantly, just as the major corporations are examining the validity of monolithic corporate identities (Ford says it must 'think global, act local') a new government is taking them on. As in so many of its initiatives, this idea is now a generation out of date. Simplistic notions of identity cannot survive the Darwinian struggle for survival in the densely nuanced Information Age. It is true that brands are increasingly important in the marketplace, but it is also becoming difficult to ascribe to them a particular *national* identity.

The realities of world business with instantaneous transfers of data and capital and global manufacturing make a mockery of olden-days nationalism. The radically designed Ford Ka is no doubt a very cool product, but is it British? Not in any very credible sense it isn't. The Ford Ka is manufactured in Spain by an American corporation using components sourced from Basildon, Belfast, Bridgend, Dagenham, Enfield, Halewood, Leamington, Treforest, Berlin, Cologne, Saarlouis, Wulfrath, Genk, Bordeaux and Valencia. It was designed in Essex and Cologne by a team of individuals sourced from more than twenty different countries.

The branding of Britain in general and Cool Britannia in particular is as misconceived as those crude notions of branding which preoccupied business in the 1980s. You cannot create brands. You can only create excellent products and support them consistently. Then after time, your brand values may evolve into something recognizable and attractive. Intangible maybe, but detectable, most certainly.

Cool Britannia is a fundamental misunderstanding of the relationship between product and brand. Genuine brand value depends on substance, on associations and expectations established over time.

It is deeply uncool to be cool. It is even more uncool for a Prime Minister to take time out from a Middle East tour, as he did in April 1998, to attack the critics of Cool Britannia. The rhetoric here was much the same as that used when Blair told the nation two months earlier to shut up and stop whining and enjoy the forthcoming Millennium Experience. Cool Britannia is not simply a generation out of date. It is embarrassing to a person of taste.

In *Democracy in America* Alexis de Tocqueville,the republican aristocrat, warned that when dictatorships emerged in democratic cultures, they would be different in character from feudalism, despotism or all the other -isms that hadn't been invented or imagined in 1839. He feared that a 'democratic' dictatorship would be 'more extensive and more mild; it would degrade men without tormenting them'. Cool Britannia is certainly degrading.

A little late in the day, the pseudo-event of Cool Britannia is being busily disavowed by the very image-builders who so opportunistically promoted it. A government that wants to dictate to the country via pseudo-events will eventually leave behind a litter of such communications catastrophes.

Chapter 4

Millennium
Muddle 1

**'If Mandy went to a voodoo sacrifice in
Brixton tonight, he'd come back saying
"we must have voodoo sacrifice in the
Dome".'**

In early 1997 I knew not much more about the Millennium project than any other person who reads the papers, although when I was surprisingly invited to be its Creative Director I had a moment's concern that the famous instant rebuttal system might be booted up to excavate a slightly sceptical comment I had made to the *Telegraph* when the idea was first advanced in 1993. One remarkable thing about the curious Millennium project is that it has none of what the consultants call 'third-party endorsement'. I was not as antagonistic as most commentators (here *The New Yorker*'s 'It's impractical, extravagant, and useless – a great European monument' was typical and so was *The Guardian*'s question 'Why should the future have to look like sets from Seventies science fiction TV programmes?'), just in possession of light scepticism.

Its early history was mixed. The spiritual origins of the Millennium Dome, circa 1993–4, are in the Liverpool Garden Festival, a flowering bud of Michael Heseltine's and something of a successful one. Like Liverpool, Heseltine's conception of the Millennium project combined the strands of inner-city rejuvenation with a commercial trade show. Birmingham had seemed the most likely (not to mention most practical) venue for the event, but Heseltine was seized by messianic vigour and saw the opportunity to extend the stalled Docklands experiment. Add to this Greenwich's symbolic significance as its site on the prime meridian and its scientific traditions of timekeeping together with Heseltine's persuasive advocacy, and by 1996 the competition had been decided in Greenwich's favour.

You could not say that this extension of Docklands was into virgin territory: the proposed site in Greenwich was a wretchedly contaminated 181-acre plot abandoned by British Gas. It was awash with toxins and for the first months of the reclamation project visitors were not allowed to wind down the windows of their cars, still less get out and breathe the air. Trucks had to go through wheelwashers lest they contaminate the neighbourhood. The costs just of cleaning up the chemical swamp are in the order of £20 million, but the clean-up can never be total or complete: a bright orange barrier layer of plastic is set just below the surface both to contain the toxins and warn men with shovels of the simmering subterranean threat. To add to the menu of carcinogenic options, a monumental exhaust for the Blackwall Tunnel rises within the perimeter of the vast structure.

There are a number of misconceptions about the Dome. The fundamental one is that it's a dome in the first place. It's not. The astonishing structure on Greenwich peninsula is in fact a tent. It's the largest cable net tent in the world, an architectural design of astonishing bravura and an engineering feat of unexampled audacity. And at £40 million the structure of the Dome is cheap: you would be delighted to have your kitchen extension built at the miserly rate of £1,300 a square metre. Yet while there is no gainsaying the drama and memorability of the pseudo-dome, it is in fact a rather old architectural concept. New technology allows more adventurous and interestingly irrational structures, just as current fashion demands them. Sir Philip Dowson, an architect whose career was spent in Ove Arup, one of the world's most distinguished firms of structural engineers, says 'It is not an intelligent building.'

And while it is true that the Dome is inexpensive, all you are getting is a lot of low-service space. Mike Davies is famously proud that the Dome structure weighs less than the air it contains, and a lot less than all the hot air surrounding it. As an architectural design, it recalls the visionary sketches made by the Archigram Group in the 1960s. This influential team of architects created the design culture in which Richard Rogers grew up: they built little, but their dramatic techno-pop visualizations of future cities powerfully informed the Rogers world-view. I don't take second place to anybody in my admiration for Richard Rogers' achievements, but the Millennium Dome *does* have characteristic flaws. Like the fabulous Pompidou Centre in Paris and the even more fantabulous Lloyd's in the City of London, the Dome was very much the building Rogers *wanted* to make rather than the building which the client *needed*. Like each of those, it is full of what Stewart Brand called 'dazzling contradictions'. Unlike those distinguished predecessors, at the time it was designed no one had a clue what was going to go inside it. Unlike those distinguished predecessors, it was also thirty years out of date. The German architect-engineer Frei Otto has been proposing similar (and some say more poetic) designs for over a quarter of a century.

And defensive arguments about the costs are larded with half-truths. Yes, it is a remarkable structure. But is it any use for the purpose intended? Only a qualified 'Maybe'. The cheapness has been achieved not simply through imaginative building design, but because as a temporary uninhabited structure the Dome does not need the expensive level of servicing a 'real' building would require. But its costs represent only a fraction of the whole Millennium pork barrel. In a telling comparison, the epochal Guggenheim Museum in Bilbao which has stimulated universal praise and admiration cost a mere £60 million. It is a permanent building which will revitalize a neglected corner of Spain in perpetuity. To give another chilling example of the wanton extravagance of the Greenwich Millennium project, the total cost exceeds that of the new Getty Centre in Los Angeles, perhaps the greatest art museum ever built.

But the architecture of the Dome itself is only a small part of the controversy about the Dome issue in general. The real controversy is about matters of style and substance: what does it mean and what is it for? No doubt that Richard Rogers saw the opportunity to employ modern architecture as a vigorous symbol of New Britain. That much would have been splendid and this was why many people genuinely thought the Dome should be left empty, as an awe-inspiring folly in the best sense of the word. The Eiffel Tower is useless (and was opposed by the great French intellectuals of the day, including Guy de Maupassant, Charles Gounod and Dumas *fils*) and that has not stopped it becoming one of the most loved 'buildings' in the world. But it's important to realize that the Eiffel Tower has achieved its profound resonance (Roland Barthes said 'It means everything') because it was associated with an astonishing exhibition. It was only when plans of how to fill the Dome began to develop that the true extent of the muddle became depressingly clear.

My first feelings were that here was an opportunity to recreate something as important as 1851. The parallels with the

Millennium Dome are remarkable. The Great Exhibition of the Industry of All Nations was a unique project of world-historical significance. In Kensington Gardens Prince Albert and his busy *consigliere*, Henry Cole, proposed a vast exhibition of manufactured goods from all over the world to give the British public and British industry lessons in taste. It also, by extension, acquired for Britain during the period when manufacturing was the essence of economic activity, symbolic 'ownership' of the idea of industrial design. The Great Exhibition was a vast popular success: Paxton's building was a world-first in gigantic pre-fabrication, and the intellectual and cultural legacy of the brief event included the establishment in South Kensington of some of the greatest universities and museums, the V&A, the Science Museum, Imperial College, not to mention the touching Albert Memorial which marks the site. Of course, plans for what became known as the Crystal Palace were met with howls of derision and boorish contumely which make today's tabloids read like Wittgenstein.

In booming biblical cadences Ruskin condemned Paxton's imaginative structure as a 'cucumber frame between two chimneys'. Popular grievances included: anxiety that the Catholic A. W. N. Pugin, architect of Parliament, might corrupt Protestants by using his medieval court as an advertisement for Popery. Protectionists said the exhibition would excite consumer demand and suck in waves of trashy foreign imports. Moralists said the simple, gay innocence of the yeomanry would be corrupted and debauched by the garish lure of such an attraction. Conservatives feared that Chartists, Socialists and Syndicalists would congregate in Hyde Park and foment bloody insurrection. Mathematicians said knowingly that the first gale would bring the iron and glass fabric tumbling down, and there were other concerns that the crowds generated by the Exhibition would lead to food shortages all over the south-east. The same crowds, it was felt, might reawaken dormant Black Death microbes. Tub-thumpers said this hubristic Victorian Tower of Babel would be bound to attract divine retribution, and the King of Prussia stopped his relatives visiting London lest they be perverted by a popular spectacle. Against all this, the contemporary polemic against the Dome seems feeble indeed.

1851 had its own trouble with the intellectual and artistic integrity of its contents: some of the more remarkable exhibits included the *char-volant*, a carriage drawn by kites; a doctor's walking-stick with integral enema, and a group of stuffed frogs, one holding an umbrella. But of course, the Great Exhibition was a huge success. At the opening on 1st May 1851 the tribulations and the sneering were forgotten in a gorgeous spectacle and Thackeray said 'It was a noble awful great love-inspiring gooseflesh-bringing sight.' Peter Mandelson routinely uses the example of 1851 to diss the Dome dissidents, saying all great projects have their critics. But he makes one big mistake, notwithstanding the stuffed frogs. In 1851 the philistines were on the outside; today it's the other way around. The Millennium Tent is a political advertisement full of what Auberon Waugh calls 'patronizing rubbish'. The man responsible for hijacking a project that could have been one of the great international world exhibitions, but is instead going to be a crabby and demoralizing theme park, is Peter Mandelson.

My own appointment as Creative Director of the Millennium occurred at the time of the 1997 election when the status of the project was in the balance. In opposition, Labour had been cool about it and after the election victory the feeling was that, with so much else to do, the new government would ditch a misconceived Conservative project, write off a few millions and avoid being mired in stale Tory goo. But, astonishingly, in a spirit of can-do post-election euphoria, possibly now recalled in sober regret, Blair committed the government to the Greenwich Millennium. That was the good news. The bad news was that the Prime Minister gave the project to Mandelson, the ex-Director of Communications for New Labour (and whose maternal grandfather, Herbert Morrison, had been the 'client' of the 1951 Festival of Britain). This confirmed suspicions that the Millennium was now politicized.

Certainly, my very first experiences showed that it was not run like the creative business it pretended to be, but as a tightly controlled function of government. The culture of the staff was overwhelmingly public sector, drawn from the civil service and local government. This mentality dominated. Even the Millennium Company's Press Officer, Gez Sagar – a shifty high priest of connivance, or an ingenious cove, depending on your point of view – had emerged from Walworth Road, the dreary headquarters of old Labour. Gez had Mandelsonian instincts about control, but lacked Mandelson's character, power and style. A lack of Mandelson's very particular character, power and style would not be considered a crippling impediment by most people, except there was always the impression that Gez Sagar not only wanted to please 'Peter', but would actually rather like to become him.

A great deal of the bad publicity surrounding the Dome is attributable to the neurotic atmosphere of furtive retraction-and-denial which characterized the New Millennium Experience Company Limited's transactions with the Press in its ever-more-desperate attempts to win public approval. Every sarky comment by a semi-literate tabloid was treated like a three-minute warning of the Apocalypse. News management is a contagion. If the Press notices that something is being covered up, the Press quite naturally gets curious. Sagar's view was that public opinion is of supreme importance, something few would care to deny. The difference between us was that I felt public opinion was best won by doing positive interesting things and promoting them with style and energy. The Millennium style is to satisfy public opinion by coercive news management, and if this calls for an armoury of Press Office cudgels and gags, then cudgels and gags will be employed.

Far better an attractive pseudo-event than a questionable real one. It is an unedifying business to witness. If public opinion thinks the Dome is a dubious venture, a lot of the blame is attributable to the style of the Press Office which creates a mood of apologetic furtiveness about every Millennium activity. Every posture required of Millennium staff is a defensive one.

The Friday of the week my appointment as Consultant Creative Director was announced, I had a long-standing commitment to take two American visitors around some of London's contemporary museums. Radio 4's *Today* programme had received the Press Release, and called me at home in the kitchen at about 7.15 a.m. I explained that I couldn't talk at the time – children's breakfast, sloshing cafetières, that sort of thing – but said I'd gladly talk again later from the car.

So I gave my first Millennium interview from a Ford Galaxy on London's King's Road. It went rather well. I was enthusiastic and said I looked forward to doing something exciting and interesting which would combine the best of art and industry in a huge popular event. Without being vainglorious, the short chat was received with good humour and interest by the *Today* team and my companion in the car, a Senior Vice-President of the Ford Motor Company in charge of Government and Public Affairs (an expert in global PR) said it was good, so I felt fine, terrific, this is a start. By the time I got back to my office, Gez Sagar was on the phone, whining and complaining that we had not discussed what I was going to say and very scratchy that I had not forewarned him. My reply was that between seven and eight in the morning on a live programme when I had scarcely been forewarned myself, Stalinist briefings were not appropriate and in any case, what was the harm as I'd only said good things. And why on earth had he issued a two-page Press Release about me if he hadn't wanted people to take an interest? Coming from a background whose horizon was universities and whose foreground included ten years working for Terence Conran, I had come to believe that the principle of good communications is that people who know what they are talking about should stand up and say it as winningly as possible. I was getting the impression that such straightforwardness did not fit well in the Millennium Muddle.

A few weeks before I first met Peter Mandelson, *The Guardian* ran a profile with a headline describing me as 'The Peter Mandelson of aesthetics'. This rather amused me, the implied diabolical mastery of my own subject being flattering. So much so that when we were eventually introduced, I mentioned the description to the Minister. He offered the very thinnest of smiles, engaged in a brief pause, dipped his head and asked if I was pleased. I didn't at the time have a response, although it is noteworthy that Mr Mandelson has not since taken up the seemingly attractive option of describing himself as the 'Stephen Bayley of Politics'. As a politician, it is inevitable that Peter Mandelson has a disposable attitude to aesthetics. With someone like myself, who regards typography as far, far more important in the general run of things than politics itself, there is potential for conflict. Alas, while it would be absurdly self-dramatizing actually to believe what the papers say, it does seem that the then Minister Without Portfolio (now elevated to the DTI, where with becoming modesty he has reverted to the pre-Heseltine title of Secretary rather than President) and I had a doomed relationship, such as it was.

Our first meeting was the day in June when Mandelson, pager attached and retinue in place, came to address the staff of the Millennium. He said something like 'I believe in art, design and excellence . . . *however,* I am a politician.' I chirrupped up something like 'So this means there are occasions when you don't believe in art, design and excellence.' People say it took minutes for the chill to leave the room.From that moment on, creativity and politics were in conflict. The project's name is typical of the futile arguments. I recommended calling the whole enterprise simply 'Millennium' since I felt that both the building and concept were big enough not to require what a lexicologist would call redundant amplification. Apart from anything else, the two 'm's of millennium offered interesting graphic opportunities with suggestions of the Roman notation for 2000. But Mandelson insisted that his new diversion be called the New Millennium Experience Company Limited. I pointed out that Experience was a corny word. We have a Cadbury's Chocolate Experience in Bournville and thirty years before we had the Jimi Hendrix Experience. I also pointed out that it was a mouthful for people to say when answering the phone – 'Good morning, New Millennium Experience Company Limited Tracy speaking how can I help no I'm sorry he's not answering' – and that the nearly fifty characters and spaces of NMEC would not fit in the window of a standard DL envelope if set in 12-point type. But that didn't matter next to the ministerial *fiat*.

Ham-fisted political interference has been continuous. Although Heseltine and Mandelson were occasionally seen together on Millennium business, the Tory origins of the project were all but forgotten. But when on occasions seen *ensemble,* the duo made an impression both hilarious and chilling, affording spectators one of the most grotesque scenes popular culture can afford. Heseltine: huge, imperious, surprisingly frail-looking, vague, insensitive, dogmatic and smug. Mandelson: slippery.

The structure of the Millennium Company is a paradigm of bad management. Although constituted as a limited liability company, the Millennium's senior staff have no relevant experience of management, still less of managing creative projects on such a huge scale. The tendency is not to solve problems as they occur, but to appoint consultants, myself included. The very same thing that makes civil servants incorruptible (their refusal to make individual decisions) disqualifies them from running a business. Add to that an interfering shareholder and you have a recipe for the unco-ordinated chaos that has mired the entire project. Instead of acting out the role of real business and reporting to the shareholder quarterly or annually, the shareholder is on the phone hourly and the pusillanimous management, hobbled by traditional Whitehall instincts, is responsive to his peremptory demands (although snide about him behind his back).

Take two well-publicized examples of Millennium Muddle: the Union Jack and Christianity. These are perfect examples of how the unreasonable creative impulse can only with difficulty work with the more pragmatic political one. Now, I happen to be extremely proud of being British and take second place to nobody in my argumentative advocacy of Britain's superiority in many of life's refinements. I think it is sensationally interesting and stimulating that the world's biggest Millennium event is happening in London. Our capital is the most exciting city in the world, not only because the ethnically British happen to be good at what the Department *für* Kultur, Media *und* Sport would call the 'creative industries', but because every Spanish film-maker, Argentinian architect, American photographer and German designer wants to work here. The Millennium had the potential to be a superb advertisement for Britain's huge contemporary competitive advantage. Union Jacks, notwithstanding my admiration for the timeless graphics of the Union flag, are redundant in this context.

Christianity is more contentious, but the creative argument would be that, of course, Judaeo-Christian theology has established our moral and justice systems which are the most decent in the world. However, a narrow denominational approach to the Millennium which involved the Established Church may alienate Jews, Hindus, Parsees, Muslims, Catholics, Vegetarians, Scientologists and Voodoo Priests. Far better to construe religion as an integrated part of a healthy culture and to ensure that Millennium activities reflect and generate the highest aesthetic and moral principles.

The Union Jack response and the Christian casuistry were impulsive responses to momentary stimuli. Mandelson wrote to *The Daily Telegraph* after some pissed-off bishops had nagged him and assured them that the 'impact of Christianity on Western civilization will be central to the Millennium Experience'. Maybe the instant rebuttal thing is contagious, but what Mandelson wrote was not true. It also indicated to anyone who knew that he had no programme whatsoever. This was why, after my final resignation, I expressed my frustration by saying:

'If Mandy went to a voodoo sacrifice in Brixton tonight, he'd come back tomorrow saying "We must have voodoo sacrifice in the Dome".'

Mandelson would do anything in the Dome which he felt would get votes. That's the degree of intellectual integrity involved.

A third example of the muddle has had no publicity at all. The Millennium (as I insisted on calling it) needed a logo and I decided to make this my first creative task. Brilliant logos have always fascinated me: the best are ingenious visual puns which manage to convey the complexities of a big organization simply and memorably. For the designer, the creative challenge is to make something novel and memorable, but which also satisfies some very severe practical points: a good logo must work in all media (from print on paper through stone carving to video), must work in all dimensions (from a tiny lapel pin to a laser light show), and must reproduce in monochrome and in colour. The option of implementing something memorable was lost when design proposals were tested on focus groups and rejected for irrelevant reasons concerned with geopolitics, not meaningful communication. A great opportunity was lost, a great designer had been rebuffed, a lot of time and money wasted and I had realised that creative autonomy meant nothing in Labour Camp's politicized Millennium.

It took a year for another graphic device to be designed. When Martin Lambie-Nairn's proposal was revealed in June 1998, it was greeted by titters and nudges. Looking like titles to a Swiss Film Festival from the 1970s, Lambie-Nairn's graphics employed a *kitsch* pseudo-Cretan steroid-pumped bronze female figure designed by Mark Reddy, who used to work for Saatchi and Saatchi, but had now retired from adland to become a Sunday sculptor of middle-brow tat. An almost identical – possibly even the very same – Mark Reddy figure had previously been used in an advertisement for a proprietary anti-angina treatment, manufactured by Roche (whose advertising account is held by Hayden). Never mind the meaningless, witless low-brow art, it was – as a corporate identity – a piece of design of stunning ineptitude with a complete lack of graphic intelligence (therefore favourably received by artless Millennium staff and the chief political shareholder). The Millennium logo is a travesty of design: it conveys no witty meaning, it will not work in all sizes, it will not work in all media and it will not reproduce effectively in different colours. At least its essential muddle reveals sympathy with the cause.

But the true muddle of the Millennium Dome, the authentic disaster of mis-management and political bungling, is in the contents. The process by which the Dome is filled is directed by EU legislation: all government contracts above a certain value have to be advertised in *The Official Journal of the European Union*. With a very few exceptions, the quality of the firms expressing interest is very low: Europe's great architects and designers have almost entirely ignored the invitation. My immediate suggestion that we re-advertise and coerce entries from the best designers was ignored. Thus, a pattern of complacent mediocrity was established and I had to accept that there was really no prospect of commissioning serious creative work. In fact, I had to accept that I had been had.

To compound the error, this same motley of smallish design consultancies, presentation companies and two or three architects of genuine quality were given briefs of baffling vagueness and asked to interpret them. No creative co-ordination of content was allowed. The problem here is simply that no designer, no matter how talented, can generate content for an exhibition: that has to be done by curators and academics. It is as absurd as asking the film crew to make a movie without a director and without a script. Hence the tepid vulgarity of some designs and contentless elegance of others.

It was at about this time that the exciting new game of surfball was invented as a remedy for the bafflingly incoherent and uncohesive contents that had been generated by this back-to-front process, described by one architectural professional who had first-hand experience as 'a disgrace'. Surfball confirmed a trend towards lowering populism, and thus a visit to Disney for the Minister without Portfolio turned what had been a mere trend into an established belief system. Just as Excalibur had rescued Labour, so a fussy little trip to the world's biggest theme park was planned to rescue the Dome. Never mind that Disney has been described as being in relation to fun 'what Velveeta is to cheese: pasteurized, processed, smooth, neat, bland, square, loved by children' (Jane and Michael Stern, *Encyclopaedia of Pop Culture*, 1992). Never mind that Disney is witlessly orthodox, culturally crude and oppressive in its Kafka-esque diminution of the individual in an overwhelming environment he cannot control. Never mind that, Disney it was to be.

A covert mission to Florida to experience at first hand Disney's supreme professionalism would have been one thing, but a formal audience with Mickey Mouse for inspirational purposes was, I felt, misjudged. Mandelson felt this too. He ran away from his accompanying photographers who tried to picture him in the embrace of the redundant rodent, although he was perfectly happy to be photographed mouse-free and on-message and at-ease in front of Cinderella's Castle. The widely published photographs of Mandy *chez* Mickey were greeted with howls of derision. Paul Goldberger, the distinguished architectural critic of *The New Yorker*, said:

> **'It may have been the most ill-advised visit of a politician to Disney World since Richard Nixon went to Orlando and uttered his famous "I am not a crook" line there.'**

Disney has been doing Disney since 17th July 1955 when Disneyland opened in Anaheim, California, and has acquired a peerless repertoire of deep, deep expertise in crowd management, entertainment systems and computerized data capture. Even if it were desirable to attempt a thin replica of Disney in Greenwich (which is a mere few hundred km from the local Euro-Disney in Marne-la-Vallée), the time available simply does not allow it. Much better, I believe that the Millennium Experience should be an elegant and economical exhibition about the world of the future, designed by the greatest architects and designers available: accessible to the public, comprehensible to the media and with technical collaboration from the world's great industries who would be involved as creative partners, not arm's-length sponsors.

Only one question needs be asked of the Millennium to expose its vulgar mediocrity, its lazy cliché and its vapid *kitsch*. Why, when the money and resources existed to hire the world's greatest architects, designers, artists, film-makers and musicians, do we have the prospect of visitors sitting on divan beds being towed around a trivial water feature listening to airport music? Why sunsets of the Serengeti with finger-painting? Laurie Lee wrote captions for the 1951 Festival of Britain and in 1938 Einstein lectured at the New York World's Fair: quality is not the enemy of popularity.

There is a simple answer to the question of why Mandelson does not seem to understand that the contents of the Dome are such an affront to educated taste. This is because Mandleson seems to have no genuine aesthetic sense, hence his inability to understand the grave artistic shortcomings of his Millennium Experience. Mandelson's 'intelligence' is often cited, but operates over such a narrow band that it begs a redefinition.

Mike Davies, the Richard Rogers partner who actually designed the Dome, said to me 'It's going to be a disaster, isn't it, Stephen?' Bill Muirhead, who had asked me to get involved in the first place, said the contents may end up looking like a 'mad woman's breakfast'. It's not going to be a disaster. Curiosity alone will guarantee high attendances, and an M. & C. Saatchi advertising budget of about £16 million will keep interest alive throughout the year. The tragedy is the lost opportunity.

Richard Rogers wrote a sad letter to me on 12th January 1998 saying:

| **'I am truly sorry that the NMEC bureaucratic**

machine has forced you to resign. The efficiency with which they muffled your voice was depressing. I now wish I had done more but we were kept apart by the gremlins.'

Paul Goldberger's perception from New York was that I had been asked to join the team 'in the hope that his presence would give the floundering project some stature' (*The New Yorker*, 27th April and 4th May 1998). Later, Fiona McCarthy, the most respected design writer in Britain, wrote 'He was the only person in the country who could have made the Dome experience work' (*The Guardia*n,6th March, 1998).

The fundamental deception of the Millennium Dome was that they said they wanted a Creative Director. They did not. They wanted to be able to say that they had a Creative Director and that was the end of it. Although I went hoarse trying to explain that you cannot be responsible for the design of something unless you are responsible for the idea that gave rise to it, this principle was ignored. So far from understanding and promoting the creative process, the procedures of the Dome are a travesty of it. Only a little less than one hundred per cent of the extraordinary community of architects, artists and designers in London feel alienated by it. Every sensible opportunity to make sense of the Dome's extravagant uselessness has been ignored. It *has* no creative direction. It is a pseudo-event.

Mandelson, for his part, in a bravura bit of spin, told *The Daily Telegraph* that I was 'never creative director in any case'. A few moments with his swanky EFS instant rebuttal software would have shown him how wrong he was.

Chapter 5

Irvine's Wallpaper

'Bad to the point of being laughable, but
not to the point of being enjoyable.'

Susan Sontag, *Notes on Camp*, 1964

It is astonishing what a large part furniture and furnishings have played in the public perception of the New Labour Government. It is without precedent. Even today, 3rd June 1998, as I sit down to assemble my notes for this chapter, I see *The Daily Telegraph* is running a story about a Foreign Office table. It says that the Foreign Secretary had to justify to the Foreign Affairs Select Committee why £50,000 had been spent on a table of white American oak with purple legs for the Cardiff summit of European ministers to mark the end of Britain's European presidency. Quite correctly, the Foreign Secretary defended the long-term value of expenditure on robust furniture. Some of us have been trying to persuade ministers to do the same for a very long time. But I wonder if the Foreign Secretary is sensitive to the associations of new furniture. Not in this case Alan Clark's classic about Michael Heseltine lacking heirlooms, but John Ruskin's remark on William Holman Hunt's Pre-Raphaelite masterpiece *The Awakening Conscience* (now in the Tate Gallery). In his 1856 *Academy Notes* Ruskin said you could tell the hero of the painting was a cad, a moral reprobate, because of 'the fatal newness of his furniture'.

It started with Terence Conran. Already when I was still in the Conran fold I can remember Terence getting a call from Michael Heseltine, who seems often to feature in furniture stories, asking him to help with government 'procurement' (a task one mischievously imagined might be better suited to a Grand Vizier recruiting for the Harem at Ephesus). This came to nothing. And most of Conran's dealings with preceding Conservative governments were equally frustrating and nugatory. For this reason Conran was understandably impressed when invited to furnish the Anglo-French summit in Canary Wharf with modern furniture. It would be cynical to say that Sir Terence was invited to design a pseudo-event. Conran has genuinely done more than anybody else in post-war Britain to raise expectations of, and enthusiasm for, design. He has harangued governments for forty years about taking an interest in design, in manufacturing and in art education. So his positive response to the invitation to make sure that Blair and Chirac were sitting on something comfortably modern (furnished at his own expense) may have seemed like an epiphany. I know Terence Conran very well and like him very much, so I asked him the question. I didn't use the term pseudo-event, but I did say (and I paraphrase):

'Isn't it much easier (not to say cynically opportunistic) to invite a well-disposed, socialist multi-millionaire to provide smart modern furniture at his own expense for a stage-managed government event than it is to (a) rehabilitate the British furniture manufacturing industry (b) stimulate better education and research in ergonomics, material science, business studies and all those other disciplines which make the Italian and the German furniture industries so successful? Isn't it much easier to spin this story to within a giddy inch of its death than it is to do something serious and real which has a genuine foundation in the future?'

Terence feels it is I who am being cynical and simply says in rebuttal (incontrovertible, as ever) that it is surely better to do this than to do nothing. Well, yes, of course, none of us objects to Britain being presented as a smart, modern place where leaders of the People are modern . . . but without forcing the point too much, an entertaining comparison can be made between Conran's enthusiastic response to a well-meaning initiative and another furniture episode characteristic of the first year of New Labour. While Terence Conran's decent, well-mannered new furniture was greeted by the Press with only mild and good-humoured mockery, Lord Irvine's restorations of his official residence provoked a hurricane of vituperation. Both philistines and aesthetes were outraged; something, I suppose we must concede, as evidence for the inclusiveness of New Labour. I would further say that the conceited and rather permanent antiquarianism of the controversial redecoration of the Lord Chancellor's apartments in Westminster are in fact more revealing of fundamental truths about New Labour than Sir Terence's temporary provision of Conran Shop stock for the Blair bottom and Chirac *cul*.

Although Lord Irvine and the Prime Minister have a close relationship, Tony Blair's sleek and refined popularity has not rubbed off on his less stylish mentor. Irvine is not well liked in the legal profession, although his huge power and influence in it prevents me from citing the well-informed source of this opinion, a normally fearless radical. The feeling is that Irvine is a beneficiary of favouritism, that he has been promoted above his merits and that, either as a symptom or a cause of this advancement, he has developed an embarrassing *hauteur*. The arrogance of the Lord Chancellor is indicated by his habit, reported by Lord Runciman a mite too enthusiastically to remove his Lordship entirely from charges of disinterest, in the *London Review of Books*, of addressing the Prime Minister as 'young Blair'. It is true that the Lord Chancellor (b. 23rd June 1940) is thirteen years older than the Prime Minister (b. 6th May 1953), but you can see how it might cause offence among the less distinguished or the less privileged.

At a bibulous dinner party given by Ronald Dworkin, Professor of Jurisprudence at Oxford, where, according to Walter Garrison Runciman, who was one of the guests 'the collective rate of encroachment on our hosts' wine supply [was] truly awesome', Irvine's loosened tongue betrayed the extent of his inflamed ambition. Runciman noted in his diary that Irvine 'is ebulliently confident of soon tasting the fruits of high office'. And, presumably, in an environment so replete with spires, his fancy turned to Gothic ornament.

The opening of the Lord Chancellor's apartments on 20th April 1998 was widely – one is tempted to say 'universally' – reported. The day after, *The Times* gleefully recounted that Norah Robinson, Lord Irvine's official Train Bearer (an essential component in the democratic apparatus of New Labour) had to keep vigilant station in front of the loo lest disrespectful reporters intrude to assess the extent of Gothic infiltration into the water closet.

How odd for the chief law official of New Labour to take such pride in Conservative nostalgia. Is there not some very odd contradiction when a New Labour Lord Chancellor with a New Labour website spends £14,000 on a repro dining table, £32,768 on eight repro mirrors, £49,773 on three repro beds, £57,233 on repro wallpaper, £24,430 on repro fabrics, £21,989 on repro carpet and £8,776 on repro crockery? It is not the cash sums that are worrying (although they concern the tabloids): decent furniture and decoration often costs serious money. The troubling thing is the *intention*. What Irvine has caused to be done is not fastidious archaeology, but a garish demonstration of camp sensibility: 'bad to the point of being laughable, but not to the point of being enjoyable'. Reproduction is *kitsch*.

How depressing to be so committed to witless pedantry. How hilarious to so pompously have misunderstood history. The apartment the Lord Chancellor occupies was intended as a simple accommodation for Black Rod: a functional room for a functionary. Under Irvine (who had earlier told the Press he felt he had something in common with Cardinal Wolsey) it has been rebranded as magnificent chambers – with embarrassing and utterly inappropriate effect. Sir Roy Strong has said:

> **'I would almost pay not to live there. It is halfway between a Victorian station hotel and a bad provincial museum.'**

But what is most revealing is how Irvine's pompous self-aggrandizing betrays a fundamental ignorance of the very history he is so keen to exploit and evoke. What has been done to his apartment in Pugin's name is a travesty of Pugin's own philosophy.

In Augustus Welby Northmore Pugin (1812–52) flowed many of the contradictory currents which animated the very deep pool of High Victorian culture. The decisive moment in his life was his conversion to Catholicism, but what he brought to Britain was a continental perspective, not from his French Protestant nobleman father, but from late German Romanticism. Friedrich Schlegel had as early as the 1830s criticized the moral emptiness of contemporary architecture. Pugin converted to Catholicism circa 1835 because he felt that his contemporary world was lacking in 'truth' and 'life'. He had a vision (which, in a different style, transmitted itself directly to William Morris and thereafter to the Bauhausmeisteren and the pioneers of Modernism) that architecture had meaning and moral content. A grand style, Pugin believed, could only be achieved if it were in the service of a belief system – Roman Catholicism.

The first of Pugin's reforming books was *Contrasts, or a parallel between the architecture of the fourteenth and fifteenth centuries and similar buildings of the present day* (1836). Here, in a challenging then-and-now format, Pugin treats architecture as a reflection of the Spirit of the Age (and finds early Victorian Britain with its factories, panopticons and crude classical styles of architecure pitiably and wretchedly wanting). To Pugin, classical architecture was an expression of a Godless utilitarianism and therefore disgusting. From his English mother, daughter of a prosperous Lincolnshire evangelist family, he perhaps acquired his taste for argument and polemic. His use of architecture as social criticism is both humorous and withering, and in his first building, his own house, St Marie's Grange at Alderbury, near Salisbury (1835), he established a vigorous style of building. With total commitment, before Ruskin, he demonstrated his conviction that art and life were a unity, best expressed in the Gothic style. Details had meaning, the whole had unfaltering moral force, and good architecture was the inevitable expression of a healthy and moral society. And the inverse held for bad architecture.

These passionate beliefs Pugin further developed in his next book, *The Principles of Pointed or Christian Architecture* (1841). He argued against flat roofs, inciting not just historical precedent and artistic principles, but using practical arguments too: in the wet north, flat roofs work less well than Gothic gables. To Pugin, all classicism tended to sham and deception. Gothic was more structurally honest.

Never mind that Charles Barry's Palace of Westminster is essentially a classical concept whose formal structure is disguised by Pugin's extraordinary programme of Gothic decoration. The result is a building of extraordinary totemic power, now a World Heritage site, an authentic manifesto of morality given architectural form. In a word, despite the apparent conflict between Barry and Pugin, Westminster has genuine artistic integrity: a remarkable synthesis of two approaches to architecture finding a sublime balance.

The refurbishment of the Lord Chancellor's apartments was, quite correctly, carried out with all the precision and authority necessary to a Grade One listed building. But while the Parliamentary Works Directorate certainly based its efforts on 'sound research', they have provided the Lord Chancellor with a fake. In the official words, it only 'reflects' the original intention. It does not reinstate, or restore, still less develop Pugin's ideas. A genuine belief in the Conran ethic would have had New Labour's Lord Chancellor in bright, optimistic, forward-looking new offices. But somehow that was never even considered.

Pugin would have deplored the conceited extravagance of the Lord Chancellor's 'reflective' scheme. Had he been alive now, Pugin would not even have encouraged a fastidious restoration, even had that been possible or advisable. To Pugin, architecture was an expression of morality and of practical possibilities. Although the image brought to mind is a comical one, Pugin would have embraced Conran. His thinking was a profound influence on the Modernist belief that you must make the best of contemporary possibilities. The blustering sham of the Lord Chancellor's apartments, in all its inappropriate and vulgar excess, would have dismayed him.

Chapter 6

In the Name of the People

'Do not attempt to operate machinery while listening to Chris Smith.'

Chris Smith has written a book. I asked Michael Sissons, one of London's (and therefore the world's) most successful literary agents, if he had read it. He sighed and said an aspirated 'No', adding 'It's published by a very good friend of mine [Matthew Evans, Chairman of Faber] . . .' and then ran out of even that amount of enthusiasm and finished the sentence by shutting his eyes and shaking his head.

Chris Smith's is not a very good book. George Walden, reviewing it in *The Sunday Telegraph* (24th May 1998) said it was an 'appalling' book, adding that:

> **'a Secretary of State for Culture has put his name to some of the most sanctimonious bilge written about arts in recent times.'**

Hilariously adding:

> **'No words can adequately convey the depths of its fatuity, except his own . . .'**

and went on to quote the wretched Smith at some length. Which I won't bother to do here, at least in not as much length. Walden explained to me that he wrote the first draft of his review when jet-lagged and bad-tempered. Because Smith is a kindly man, he briefly reconsidered his tone when he felt better- natured and more alert. But he decided against it. Smith may himself be a kindly man, but the book is pernicious in its crassness.

Creative Britain, as Smith's book is called, is indeed appalling. It is ham-fisted in style, written as though English was not the Secretary of State's first language, although he does demonstrate a wide programme of reading when he declares, in a wince-inducing expression, that 'we [as a nation] do appear to be rather good at writing'. It is dull, unoriginal, uncreative, repetitious, platitudinous, condescending, dreary, clichéd and patronizing. In addition it is horribly over-stuffed with untested assumptions and the sort of unacknowledged scissors-and-paste work which researchers provide for lazy ministers.

I heard Smith talk at the Thirty Club, a private dining club for advertising professionals which meets at Claridge's. Since the Secretary of State has (apparently) ignored the Thirty Club's convention of not reporting its transactions by publishing the text of his address in *Creative Britain*, I see no reason why I should not do the same. I noted at the time the dismaying complacency, the soporific lack of edge. 'Do not,' I scribbled on my menu 'attempt to operate machinery while listening to Chris Smith.'

On many substantial issues, well-informed people do not take issue with Smith. There is no doubt that the technical achievements of the twentieth century confound conventional definitions of 'culture'. I am not a conservative. When Santayana wrote that 'culture is on the horns of a dilemma: if profound and noble it must remain rare, if common it must become mean', he had simply not anticipated the possibilities of the century. Art is fugitive and takes different forms in different periods. As Gore

Vidal explained: 'As a source of interest for the serious, film has replaced the novel, as the novel replaced the poem . . . The half-serious reader of yesteryear is now the film-buff' (*Times Literary Supplement*, 22nd–28th June 1990).

Aldous Huxley once said that speed was the only sensation *unique* to the twentieth century: even flight had been known to Enlightenment balloonists. Huxley did not expand this curious insight into an examination of how speed affected the arts. Movies, rock music and industrial design are the distinctive cultural forms of the modern age and each depends on a (metaphorical) interpretation of speed. Most of all with industrial design. Mass production is based on a virtual circle of high volume and low cost which require uniformity of design. Henry Ford's 'Any colour as long as it's black' was another way of saying 'No scope for variations.'

So, the creative achievements of the century are based not on craftsmanship, exclusivity, rarity or preciousness. On the contrary, the extraordinary disciplines of designing for mass production and the extraordinary productive achievements of industry (16 million Volkswagens, 24 million Toyota Corollas, for instance) mean that the intrinsic value of twentieth-century design is low: manufactured cost plus a profit margin. But, equally, the same disciplines mean that success depends on getting the idea absolutely right in the first place.

Which in turn means that the very best twentieth-century design makes beautiful things available cheaply. This is a very good thing. It's what the portentous language of a polytechnic lecturer would call the aestheticization of the object and the democratization of luxury. Put more persuasively, modern technology allows the creation of an inexpensive (indeed, disposable) razor and pen superior in performance to those available in Versailles to the Sun King. The very existence of Bic and Pentel puts traditional ideas about collecting, when applied to the twentieth century, under scrutiny.

But at the same time, the most successful industrial designs acquire huge symbolic power. The Coke bottle is at least as powerful and moving a symbol of American values as Jefferson's Monticello. Equally, a 1957 Chevrolet Bel-Air is at least as vigorous and memorable an expression of American culture as the preening gallery world of SoHo. Kurt Vonnegut described modern art as a conspiracy between 'clever parasites and millionaires to make poor people seem stupid'. No one ever said this about industrial design: the '57 Chevy and the Coke bottle and the Bic razor make poor people feel terrific. Today, all consumers are collectors. Andre Malraux's 'museum without walls' has arrived in a way he had scarcely anticipated. Traditional craftsmen and artists may still exist, but they spend their careers pursuing medieval status relics.

But because aesthetics is now in the marketplace does not mean that there are no aesthetic standards, unless – as the Secretary of State possibly believes – you believe the People are morons. There are hierarchies of excellence in design and rock and movies which are just as susceptible to intelligent critical analysis as the 'old' culture. It is a fraudulent swindle for a Minister of Culture to suggest otherwise. Certainly distinctions between pop and classical are now very blurred and no one doubts that certain 'pop' musicians attain the very highest standards and, as William Mann so controversially suggested in *The Times* on the release of 'Sergeant Pepper' in 1967, there is no reason to be embarrassed by comparison of the best 'pop' songwriters with, say, Schubert. That's an argument that's been won long ago. But there is a problem with Oasis. Or at least, with Oasis's yobbish, simian, leering, foul-mouthed songwriter and guitarist sharing a glass of People's champagne at Downing Street with the Prime Minister. It is not just the problem that, as one young television producer told me, 'seeing the Prime Minister hugging a rock star is as embarrassing as watching your father trying to boogie'. It is not because Oasis is, or rather was, a popular band. Great art is almost always *eventually* popular, but that is not to say that what is popular is necessarily great art. Oasis certainly was not. Oasis was always second or third rate. The problem with the Department of Culture, Media and Sport is that it doesn't seem to have any means of distinguishing good from bad.

It is possible to attempt a methodology for determining high and low culture. It is not foolproof, but it is fun:

High culture

- Interest in creative process and symbolism
- Preference for experimentation
- Introspection preferred to action
- Accepts different levels of meaning

- Expects consideration of philosophical, psychological and social issues

Upper-middle culture

- A less literary verbal culture
- Figurative and narrative art preferred, especially if illustrative of individual achievement or upward mobility
- Enjoys nineteenth-century art and opera, but not early music or contemporary art

Lower-middle culture

- Form must unambiguously express meaning
- Demands conclusions
- Unresolvable conflicts not made explicit
- Interested in performers, not writers or directors
- Influenced by word-of-mouth judgement

Low culture

- No concern with abstract ideas: form must be entirely subservient to content
- Demands crude morality with dramatic demarcations, but usually limited to family or individual problems
- Performer is paramount; enjoys vicarious contact with 'stars'.
- Considers ornateness attractive

Thus Herbert J. Gans in *Popular Culture and High Culture* (1974). With his and his government's taste for Oasis, Elton John,

EastEnders and the films of David Puttnam in mind, you will draw your own conclusions about where Professor Gans would categorize the Secretary of State for Culture, Media and Sport.

Arts and culture are not the same thing. Culture is no concern of the state, although we have seen that authoritarian states often like to recruit the arts in their cause. However, there are plenty of intelligent things a capable Minister of Culture could find to do, such as ensuring that the great institutions which define traditional civilization are kept in good order, not simply to buttress the despised elitism of quality, but to provide a basis against which genuine creatives might react. As David Boaz says in *Libertarianism* (1997), because of the sacred power of art 'we dare not entangle it with coercive government power'. And the classic libertarian extension of this is to argue that there should never be censorship, never be regulation and never any subsidy of art. Genuine art might be gay, masochistic, anarchic and politically incorrect in any way you want to imagine. That is why governments have such difficulty with art and why the Arts Council is in such terminal confusion.

The Arts Council was an invention of John Maynard Keynes. In 1946 there was a genuine feeling of national unity. Via a personal trust fund (an effective and independent form of state subsidy) he personally established an arts theatre in Cambridge. Deep divisions and conflicts. Keynes was adamant that if the state wanted to support the arts then it must support the high arts, the ones which New Labour considers elitist: a scattergun term of PC derision.

Keynes wanted cosmopolitan artistic excellence. Here the genie of popularization crept out of the bottle. You can make the excellent popular, but you cannot necessarily expect what is popular to be excellent. Here is the central conundrum. Since Keynes, the Arts Council has struggled, often rather unsuccessfully, to come to terms with Santayana's schism between high and low, of trying to manage the unmanageable. The problem is simple, but insoluble, and can be briefly stated. If something is popular, then it does not need subsidy. If unpopular, it is hard to justify its support from public funds.

Keynes had this very debate with John Christie who, after the war, wanted Britain to have a *Volksoper*. The belief here was not in some ghastly *kitsch heimatlich* representational panto, but in the well-meaning sense that Christie thought that the canon of great opera could be genuinely popularized. The answer was yes, well, maybe. It rather depends on your definition of popularity and if summer parties for GKN and Sainsbury's directors are included. Britain never got a *Volksoper*, although the Arts Council spends £120 million a year on the Royal Opera House. Christie, of course, went on to found Glyndebourne. It is not that GKN and Sainsbury's directors are not people . . . but you can sense the potential for confusion and conflict.

It is one thing to stimulate creativity and provide certain of the resources creative people need to flourish, not least an agreeable tax regime which stimulates patronage and largesse. But a cultural policy is a hamfisted way of handling creativity – and bound to thwart it: the more so when that cultural policy has a significant economic component, as Smith insists it must. This can lead to all sorts of absurdities: and it does.

Art must be subversive, which is just one of many reasons why it cannot properly be the province of government. As David Runciman said:

> **'It is the difference between a government that wishes to "further", say, what Terence Conran has achieved, and a government that seeks to help individual designers escape from what Terence Conran may have done to the marketplace. It is not that the former shouldn't happen, but it shouldn't happen with money that might be spent on the latter.'**

But art under a dictatorship can never ever be experimental – especially if it has to make money. The Arts Council, in uneasy relationship with the mighty Department of Culture, Media and Sport struggles to accommodate this. However, a People's Chairman has been appointed to look after the interests of Labour Camp. He is called Gerry Robinson. In a letter to *The Times* (27th May 1998), the Arts Council Chairman, Gerry Robinson, clarified his new strategy for dealing with the confused and demoralized Arts Council. The style of the letter was that of an office memorandum in which the cynical banality of 'portion control' (the stuff of Mr Robinson's ugly catering business) was replaced by another cynical banality, the 'artform'. The literary style of this letter was like the cleaning rota for the lavatories of a bingo hall. How utterly baffling that the man responsible for signing such a leaden Stakhanovite letter is now in charge of the organization once run by the elegant J. M. Keynes.

Art under New Labour is defined as a lowering populism. Sir Roy Strong believes that Blair's Government is determined to see the end of the continuous aristocratic culture which has defined British life. They are, he says 'crude, crude, crude'. Museums are too expensive and olden-days fine art is surely elitist. The only museum to enjoy preferment is the Tate Gallery where the director, the son of an old-Labour peeress, is ostentatiously committed to New Pseudo-Events. In this context the Turner Prize deserves a special commendation. It is the paradigm of what Brian Sewell calls the Serota Tendency (as if it were a clinical depravity): a humourless, uncritical acceptance of novelty, irrespective of aesthetic value and unexamined by firm judgments about value or meaning. Serota was a champion of Damien Hirst and it is no surprise to see one of Hirst's paintings on the jacket of *Creative Britain*.

Hirst is a publicist and prankster (and nowadays a restaurateur) of protean genius, but irrelevant as an artist except in the purely historiographical sense. Hirst is himself a brilliant pseudo-event. And Hirst was, of course, a former winner of the notorious Turner Prize. Smith says the Turner Prize is a good thing because it generates 'public profile' and he trills that 'it goes out on television'. The Turner Prize is, in fact, also a classic pseudo-event in that it exists for the media and for no one else except its own beneficiaries. The quality of the work on show brings to mind Robert Hughes' comments on the New York Whitney Biennial:

> **'a sprawling, dull piece of documentation like a school pinboard project.'**

(*The Culture of Complaint*, 1993)

In none of his semi-literate ramblings (where 'artwork' is a solecism for 'work of art') does the Secretary of State for Culture, Media and Sport indicate any critical ability, any willingness to quantify and evaluate. Still less is there any evidence of aesthetic sense. The Tate is good because it is uncomfortably full most of the time. But what is the quality of the experience the jostled visitor gets? It is probably elitist even to ask.

In the People's Britain where *EastEnders* is uncritically advanced as 'art', the conventional theatre is as neglected as museums. Even the avant-garde conventional theatre is treated badly by Labour Camp. Stephen Daldry, who might, if he'll excuse me for saying so, in a different age have been considered a prime candidate for Chairmanship of Luvvies for Labour, says from his regular table at The Ivy:

> **'Old Labour was fine because while they didn't much care for theatre, they did enjoy active subsidy. Even the Tories were fine because while they deplored subsidy, they did rather like the glamour of a good first night, so you could do business with them.'**

The problem as Daldry sees it is New Labour, which likes neither subsidy nor art. Chris Smith's idea of a Prime Minister who defends 'high' culture is one who goes to see *King Lear* at the Cottesloe after hanging out with Oasis. Cool stuff. Alternative evidence for Smith's mistaken understanding of 'high' culture is that the release of the insane plans to put the Royal Opera House, the Royal Ballet and the English National Opera under one roof were originally scheduled for release during the World Cup, so that news of a budget production of *The Makropulos Case* might go undetected amid excitement about the half-time score of the Italy versus Cameroon match.

Music has suffered too. Because it is expensive and difficult, it is being systematically extirpated from the National Curriculum. When Sir Simon Rattle complained about this savage philistinism, his acquiescence was sought by the promise of future influence. The same controls were applied to Richard Rogers. Instead of allowing him his role as a brave agitator and outspoken popular champion of architecture and the environment, a position his strong views and unrivalled experience qualify him admirably to fill, Rogers' own acquiescence has been acquired by being offered the Chairmanship of the Urban Task Force. If it gets anything done, the Urban Task Force will be a very good thing. If it doesn't, an architect of genius with the potential to become a great social critic will have been muted. Asked to explain, a source formerly close to Rogers simply said 'He has become greedy.'

Despite the status which Richard Rogers enjoys, architecture as a whole is not understood. There are no two things more fundamental to civilization than building and diet, since the quality of the environment and of the food we eat determines more abstruse matters such as happiness and prosperity. Get architecture and food right and all else follows, but while such a radical programme might have been a real cause for a Department of Culture, Media and Sport (a name chosen because it was more 'forward looking' than National Heritage) to take up, it has neglected to do so. Simple changes to the tax regime could stimulate consistent and decent refurbishment of old buildings, just as they could discourage wanton development of greenfield sites. But to invigorate the environment in this way and secure long-term benefits might lose short-term votes. Besides, if focus groups indicated that the next election would be won by concreting over the Vale of Evesham, the concrete would be ordered tomorrow.

Meanwhile, the groovily abbreviated DCMS publishes lists of celebrity architects; and Robin Cook, one gathers, while not a noted aesthete in other aspects of his conduct, has photographs of remarkable new British buildings on what was once Palmerston's Foreign Office wall (fastidiously restored to High Victorian splendour) – but the architectural profession feels slighted. Smith scores an hilarious own-goal when he writes that 'British architects are being called on to design many of the great new monuments around the world.' He is right: just look at Berlin and Marseilles and Shanghai. But they are not being asked to design the great new monuments Britain deserves. Just look at Manchester, Leicester and Southampton. Clearly, Mark Fisher, then Minister of the Arts (and a genuine enthusiast), had difficulty in persuading his Pooterish superiors that architecture matters. *Item*: the Millennium Village has been designed not by a 'New' British architect, but by an octogenarian.

Fashion, because it photographs well and is widely reported in the tabloids, is better understood and more vocally supported, although while Galliano and Alexander McQueen may well be uncomfortable but authentic talents, there is a suspicion that Stella McCartney's qualifications lie more in the area of acquired celebrity than of creativity. We have seen that a definition of 'low-brow' is the taste for 'vicarious contact with celebrities'. Her election to the Panel 2000 committee of cool was, one suspects, a covert means of acquiring her father for Labour Camp. Sir Paul McCartney had all the apparent credentials: successful, non-aligned, but politically correct. Stella McCartney resigned from Panel 2000 in late June 1998. The assumption was that she felt her image had been exploited, but her opinion had not been sought. Here again is the schism between easy access to style and the more troubling investigation of content.

This is typical of the superficiality which characterizes New Labour's understanding of art and creativity. While 'economic value' is central to Chris Smith's justification of culture, he has an imperfect understanding of just where genuine cash value lies in the world of fashion design. When he writes 'British designers have taken charge in many of the top continental houses' he should check who actually is the Président-Directeur-Général of Chloe and then ask himself if he fully appreciates the significance of tokenism. John, Alex and Stella are like outboard motors. To say they have 'taken charge' is like saying the British design graduate who details Audi doorhandles has 'taken charge' of the Volkswagen Group.

On design matters the Secretary of State is confused by half-truths fed by the Design Council. It is true that the huge Korean *chubol*, Daewoo, designs its cars at the old IAD premises in Worthing, and that drawings are zapped down ISDN lines to Seoul; but as soon as the Korean currency collapses (which I think was last week), then suddenly a coruscating design facility that is not connected to a manufacturing resource becomes an embarrassment. Again, it is true that Britain does have world-class expertise in computer graphics – although it is worth being a cautionary spoilsport to say that this expertise depends on hardware which no British company has the ability to manufacture.

Publishing is another matter. Yes, the English language is a national asset of immeasurable value, but on the other hand the biggest publisher of English-language books is the *Verlagsgruppe* of Bertelsmann, and the fact that Bertelsmann executives hold their board meetings in English should not be a source of pride: it simply means that ownership of the English language is passing into the hands of foreigners. It is true that 80 per cent of global digital communication is in English, but it's *American* English. In automotive design, fashion, film and publishing, you do not have to be a Marxist to understand how important it is to own the means of production. Smith waffles on about 'economic value', but simply doesn't know what it really means. Take his beloved film industry. £750 million would create and endow both an impressive film school and the distribution company so desperately needed if American monopoly of the popular cinema is ever to face competition. The problem is, you can't interview or photograph or hug a distribution company.

But we do have the Creative Industries Task Force, on which sits a shirtmaker and a fat thirty-something television entrepreneur, intimate of Mandelson's, who gave the world *The Big Breakfast*, a show so dumbed-down it can't pick itself up. No one has bothered to think about how very distasteful creative people find any form of collective activity, but never mind: this is New Britain and we are re-writing the rules. This cool task force is a joint effort of the Department of Trade and Industry, the Foreign Office, the Treasury, the Department of Education and Employment, and the DCMS. Words alone cannot express just how stimulating such a collaboration sounds. As if such a task force were not in itself pure East Germany, in the name of the people we also have in Tom Clarke a Minister for Film and Tourism. Next, a Ministry for Private Views and Parties.

Smith's view of the world is ridiculously patronizing. Yes, he beams, poor people can enjoy Elgar and Puccini. He condescendingly cites the Black influence on contemporary music, apparently oblivious to Stravinski and Motown. He evokes Roni Size (a jungle DJ specializing in Postmodern layers of beat with hectic mid-range, a winner of the Mojo Best Newcomer Award of 1998) and Jazzie B (the genius of soul2soul) without seeming to know who they are or just what they do. In his pitiable flirtation with street life, Smith is reminiscent of that story about Jack Lang who, when French Minister of Culture, asked a black girl if she was enjoying an exhibition of popular art. 'Just because I'm black,' she sneered, 'does not mean I've sold out to subculture.' At least Jack Lang was responsible for some real *grands projets*.

New Labour's approach to the arts has achieved the astonishing double of alienating both hip street culture and the high culture of the established institutions. Profound ignorance is disguised by an awful blokish populism. It has dabbled in parties and entertainment in pursuit of cheap access to glamour. There is no aesthetic vision, no hint of standards of excellence. Everything is lost in a coarse muddle where fame is the sole criterion for membership and accessibility the sole criterion of quality. Instead of tackling the mechanics of government, Chris Smith preferred to make a complete arse of himself and go to the Cannes Film Festival. Smith has a budget of nearly one billion pounds, but is, according to A. N. Wilson, 'A philistine who talks twaddle and does nothing' (*The Standard*, 11th June 1998). This is fair comment.

But Cannes gave him a moment of fame. No need to go to the trouble of making up a pseudo-event, here is one somebody prepared earlier. Celebrity (from the Latin *celebritas*, 'multitude') is the phenomenon of being much talked about. Originally it meant a condition, not a personality. Chris Smith is a New Labour Camp celebrity. George Walden asked if it was elitist to expect a modicum of respect in a Secretary of State. Yes it is. And the request has been ignored.

Chapter 7

Spin

'Political language . . . is designed to make lies sound truthful and murder respectable, and to give an appearance of solidity to pure wind.'

George Orwell

Peter Mandelson is a spin doctor. But who is he and what is that?

Mandelson, according to Gore Vidal, has the 'insolent manner of one born to the ruling class but three'. The great American essayist and novelist may have confused effect with cause. Mandelson is the chief spin doctor of New Labour, a man one journalist described as a 'cold-eyed, rootless operator, a scheming corridor cowboy who has sold the soul of the Labour Party to get what he wants'.

When Mandelson arrived at the beginning of the New Labour project, the membership was what Barry Delaney, an advertising professional, describes as 'dim, politically correct amateur Trots in fairisle sweaters'. Mandelson professionalized this shoddy team. He turned his Millbank HQ into a churning multitude of talented media folk, each one of whom was responsible to him. Mandelson understands the media, although the feeling always was that while at LWT his interest was not in acquiring even the most basic of the limited repertoire of technical skills necessary to television production, but in acquiring (in this most appropriate of circumstances) a network of his own. One can only guess about the amount of influence personal events have had in this obsessive process: young Mandelson learnt of his grandfather's death from an ITN Newsflash, which may have caused a permanent and damaging short-circuit between image, emotion and control.

In an age of pseudo-events, he who controls the image has his fingers on the buttons of power. Mandelson's fingers were everywhere. While the promotion of the 1987 election had been left to old Labour's chosen agency, by 1997 Mandelson was completely in control. You can see how Gore Vidal might have been confused. Mandelson is manipulative and independent: it is often said that while there is a Mandelsonian style (furtive, sly, threatening, clever, smarmy), there are no Mandelsonites. It is not only the researchers and journalists who are ruthlessly orchestrated, it is politicians too. Mo Mowlam once remarked: 'I really am pleased to be doing this for the BBC. Usually Peter only lets me do Sky.'

But Mandelson's star has risen only lately. Under John Smith he was regarded (by someone understandably reluctant to be identified) as 'a lowly worm'. The distinguished journalist, Lucia van der Post, said he was 'icy, supercilious, dismissive, rude'. I repeated this comment to another distinguished journalist who quickly retorted 'No, that's *much* too cosy a description.' For someone so sensitive about appearances, he seems bizarrely insensitive about his behaviour and judgments. While, perhaps, not a lady's man in the old-fashioned sense, he routinely offends women dinner guests by his refusal to engage with anyone who does not offer a political advantage. But then, he accepts the gift-in-kind of a car loan from night-club owner Jamie Palumbo. Mandelson, the man from the Ministry of Soundbites, broke no rules by using transport provided by the proprietor of the Ministry of Sound, although many thought it an odd error of judgment, as Palumbo has made more enemies than he has friends. To savour the oddity, you have only to imagine, say, Michael Howard electioneering in a white stretch limo – complete with shag-pile seats, TV antenna, jacuzzi and wet-bar – sponsored by Peter Stringfellow.

With his smugly declared preference for Classic FM in the car, Mandelson fell unknowingly into a trap laid for him by Reggie Nadelson, a New York journalist whose recent evolution into crime writer has made Mandelson a fan. Anyway, it was Reggie who defined a certain musical style as 'classics for dummies'. Quite. Mandelson also enjoys the slightly smutty drawings of Chris Orr, drawn for Ministerial delight from the Government Art Collections. Adding to his belief that Mandelson has no aesthetic sense, Roy Hattersley said he was 'not much of a reader, in fact I don't think he reads at all.'

John Smith himself had a shrewd appreciation of Mandelson's manipulative qualities, saying he was so 'devious he would one day disappear up his own something or other'. The myth is that Mandelson pulls the strings. There are people who think he may even write Blair's speeches, although those in a position to know are sceptical. According to Nicholas Jones, Alistair Campbell, who knows about writing, said 'Writing was never his strong point . . . he had to look to friends to help him out, know what I mean?' But Mandelson's authority depends on his having 'the ear (and the mouth) of the Prime Minister', as one of Blair's media advisers told me. Maybe he has metaphorical possession of other body parts too. Above all, Mandelson can, to use the wonderful expression of Lester Bookbinder, 'turn crap into mediocrity'.

William Rees-Mogg wrote a brilliant character sketch of Andrew Neil which strikes me as almost perfectly applicable to Peter Mandelson. He said he was 'intelligent, but not perceptive, kindly [I'm not absolutely certain about this bit myself] but a bully, honest, but not scrupulous, a winner who sees himself as a loser, shrewd, but gullible' (*The Times,* 2nd November 1996).

But what is spin? It has its place in the language and techniques of paid-for communications – which is to say, in the history of organized lying. It is part of the poetics of disinformation. The word does not occur in Stuart Berg Flexner's classic of American demotic, *I Hear America Talking* (1976), but by the time Joe Klein's satire of the 1992 Democratic Campaign, *Primary Colors* (1997), was published, people are going off to the spin room as often as the President is . . . well, never mind.

The earliest reference to spin doctoring, according to Dr Emma Lenz, Senior Assistant Editor (New Words) of the *Oxford English Dictionary*, is from Saul Bellow's 1977 Jefferson Lectures (published in *It All Adds Up*, 1994). Bellow says:

> **'Success today is in junk bonds, in hype, in capturing the presidency itself with the aid of spin doctors.'**

Propinquity to junk bonds establishes a nice moral equivalence for Mandelson's spinning. But the source of the expression is in wholesome sport. The Toronto *Globe & Mail* explained that the political noun phrase comes from 'baseball where pitchers put spin on a ball to control its direction' (24th October 1988).

The *Oxford English Dictionary* Addition Series, Vol. 1 (1993) defines spin as 'bias or slant'. Political material has to be weighed and assessed in terms of fact versus spin. Spin is a part of the vocabulary of authority. The rattle of a stick in a swill bucket. Organized lying. Turning crap into mediocrity. More particularly, the enthusiastic import of this Americanism is yet more evidence of Creeping Clintonization. The old-fashioned 'discussion group' was felt to lack gravitas in New Britain and had to be replaced by the more sinister and scientific focus group (which sounds like an Orwellian or Koestleresque function under bright lights in white-tiled rooms).

Advertising as a whole is bedevilled by focus groups. Their defenders cite the advantages of having personal opinions as an alternative to desiccated quantifiable feedback. Detractors of focus groups cite it as absurd that six indolent housewives in the provinces can determine the fate of a washing powder, a car and a tampon. Still, focus groups sound modern. Their influence might be seen in the recent New Labour party political broadcasts, where content was dumbed-down to a stultifying banality so as not to offend. However, these were certainly an improvement on the 1987 party politicals, especially the one directed by Hugh Hudson where Neil Kinnock walked on a cliff-top. Sound of gulls and surf. The old-Labour leader mused that he was the 'first Kinnock in a thousand generations to go to University'. This was an extraordinary claim since, at average lifespans, there have only been about twenty-four generations of Kinnocks since the founding of Oxford. The assumption must be that either audience or production team – not to mention leader – was very dumb indeed, or that those earlier 976 generations of Kinnock were extremely precocious breeders.

All manner of absurdities occur when modern communications overwhelm politics. To put it no more extremely: moral ambiguities become compounded. In the same way, old-fashioned organized lying had to be replaced by New Spin. Defenders of spin include, quite naturally, one feels, the government's media adviser, Chris Powell of agency BMP DDB Needham. Powell says:

> **'Spin is just managing the media. You'd be daft not to.'**

Well, I don't know. It's a short step from managing news to inventing it. The addendum of the pseudo-scientific 'doctor' is, again, typical. It dignifies the disreputable.

Spin became a part of our lives when the speed of news started to blur fact and opinion. The first American newspaper editor was Benjamin Harris, whose *Publick Occurrences Both Forreign and Domestick* appeared in its first edition in 1690. Harris promised an edition of news every month, or more often only if 'any Glut of Occurrences happens'. In those days it was God, not the Devil, who made news, and it was the journalist who reported it.

Spin operates in that momentary space between event and the account of it. Since 1690 we have seen the slow evolution from the diligent reporter who could sniff out a good story to the manipulation and then the actual creation of news. John Birt, creator of New BBC, and Mandelson have a shared intellectual heritage. Any listener to, say, Radio 4 News knows that nowadays the bulk of the content is not reportage or analysis, but a form of prediction based on press releases.

It will soon be even easier for Mandelson and his colleagues to send stories spinning in any direction as they now possess an unusual degree of influence in a national newspaper. The *Daily Express* has for some time been an interest of Mandelson's, as he slyly revealed in his 'My Media' column in *The Guardian*. Just weeks later, after Labour-loving, money-broking Lord Hollick had assumed the role of proprietorship to complement his well-established facts of ownership, Mandy was able give form to that curiosity when he was alleged to have interfered with and reversed the planned appointment of Paul Routledge as that paper's Political Editor. In this he may have been aided by the presence in the *Express* building of Philip Gould, a penumbral but ever-present figure in New Labour. If you call Labour HQ and ask for Philip Gould, a receptionist will cheerfully tell you 'Oh, you'll find him at the *Express*.'

Gould has started up various agencies and folded them into bigger ones. He works unpaid. Described by one very senior advertising figure in terms that were patronizing and unflattering, Gould (whose wife, Gail Rebuck, Managing Director of publishers Random House, may have helped support his unpaid political habit) had created the notional Shadow Communications Agency around the 1992 election. It was after years of hanging around, being available to add a degree of communications professionalism to the evolution of New Labour, that Gould got his big break and happened to be the one who was sent to monitor Clinton's 1992 campaign. Now installed in the *Daily Express* building in a collaboration with NOP (doing what was described to me, by someone who doesn't want to be named, as 'focus groups with trade unions, that sort of thing'). Although I last met Gould in the kitchen of a mutual friend, he refused to contribute any comment to this book. His preference for secretiveness allows Peter Mandelson to acquire a reputation for being an all-powerful image-builder.

Gould's presence in the *Express* building indicated it was New Labour territory. Although Mandelson explicitly denied any interfering role in any appointment in a letter to *The Spectator* (23rd May 1998), the following week's issue of the paper made it absolutely clear that the Minister without Portfolio had been in the *Express* building at the very time when the invitation to Routledge was being rescinded. This proves nothing, but leaves many questions unanswered. The fascinating prospect is of the old voice of lower-middle (and emphatically Tory) England being creatively manipulated by New Labour. A key feature of Derek Draper's sacking from his weekly political column in the *Express* was his claim – at once self-aggrandizing and self-destructive – that he used to fax his copy to Mandelson at the Cabinet Office for vetting before publication. If true, this would break a fundamental convention of journalism. Pseudo-events and their spin doctors may now have a medium all of their own.

The metaphors of spin apply perfectly to the Ferris Wheel, a British Airways Millennium project for the South Bank. That the idea of a Ferris Wheel – first seen at the great 1893 Chicago Exhibition – will be exactly 107 years old at the dawn of the Millennium has not deterred official spinners from trumpeting British Airways' £26 million commitment to the revival of such an antiquity. However, it is an interesting gloss on current ideas of exactly what the nation should expect from a showcase that the only engineering concern capable (or perhaps just *willing*) to attempt the realization of this popular spinning attraction was Mitsubishi. Typical of all Dome-related stories, the budget allowed for the Ferris Wheel is now said by the Japanese to be inadequate for the dimensions of the task.

But most magnificently, the metaphors of spin apply perfectly to the fictional concept of surfball, intended to enliven activities in the Millennium Dome. Here indeed is a piece of work. The phenomenon of surball alone would justify the polemic of this book: surfball is pure pseudo-event, a case study in spin doctoring. I was around in late 1997 when it was invented. A team of middle-ranking, demoralized consultants and officials of the Millennium Company were very much under the gun to demonstrate the lively, forward-looking, stimulating and imaginative diversions available within the Dome. Engaging the higher cerebral functions for only a fraction of a second, one of their number came up with 'surfball', an apparently new coinage whose components hinted at a combination of the Americanisms so admired by New Labour together with the gruffly proletarian reference to a round plaything. I well recall the glee with which this crass idea was picked up.

Peter Mandelson took surfball to a Commons Select Committee on 2nd December 1997 and explained that 'surfball is the sport of the twenty-first century', a view endorsed by the Prime Minister, a tennis player, in the *Standard* on 19th December 1997, although no one anywhere knew what it was or what

Blair's announcement really meant. Then Austin Mitchell discovered through Parliamentary Questions that surfball did not actually exist, except as the name of an entirely unrelated US computer product. Surfball is a classic pseudo-event.

The journalist Richard Heller wrote to Peter Mandelson on 24th May 1998 asking him to explain. Heller wanted to know:

- What are the rules?
- Is it a team or an individual sport?
- What is the scoring system?
- Does it need umpires or referees?
- What equipment is required and what is the playing area?
- What physical and mental skills are involved?
- Will it teach co-operation, sportsmanship and discipline?
- Will it encourage training, application and social life?
- Is it a spectator sport?
- Does it lend itself to international competition?
- Will it offer possibilities for career development in coaching and management?

Well, in the last case, probably not. In Labour Camp, projects cannot be submitted to rational analysis. All surfball could teach was spin. It was an opportunistic deception. Surfball was a sham: pure, cynical misinformation. It never existed, except in a memo. Mandelson defending a pseudo-event produced a masterpiece of spin. He was forced to explain in the Commons that surfball, previously announced with utter conviction as the sport of the twenty-first century (and supported not only by the Prime Minister, but also by MPs Gerry Steinberg and Claire Ward) was in fact only 'illustrative'. Such a technique of disavowal could be put into service to beautify any ugly lie. Never mind that Mandelson's own agent, Stephen Wallace, was telling people that surfball was 'the way forward' and John Fitzpatrick, MP for Poplar, believed it would have a role in urban renewal: surfball was fiction. The evasion employed that 'design proposals were at a very early stage' was not even true. It was a desperate con to woo the media. Maybe in time the 1997 Manifesto can also be dismissed as a fiction, intended only for 'illustrative' purposes.

Spin, evasion, euphemism, distortion (invest not spend) are a part of a system of control that began with Excalibur. It is not new. Spin is a form of organized lying. Rather as 'social security' sounds more agreeable than 'state charity', so pseudo-events have their own history. A government obsessed with appearances has intellectual credentials that go all the way back to the early history of public relations. The father of the PR profession was Edward L. Bernays, who published his book, *Crystallizing Public Opinion*, in 1923. It was Bernays' belief that in the interests of your clients you should not sit around idly and wait for something interesting to occur, rather you had to 'make news happen'. These arguments were later enhanced in *Public Relations* (1952) and *The Engineering of Consent* (1955) which Bernays edited.

Somewhere in the New Labour vision of the future, with all its vast perspectives, there must be a dark little cloud of hubris. This was sensed by the comic, *2000AD*, which has a cartoon character, Britain's first bionic Prime Minister, B.L.A.I.R. 1. He has the strength of fifty men, a threatening smile and privileged access to an awesome form of artificial intelligence called Doctor

Spin. Interestingly, 43 per cent of readers wanted him killed off, perhaps on account of the following blasphemy. In a little speech bubble B.L.A.I.R.1 has a conversation with the Divinity:

> 'Just who do you think you are anyway, creep? God? Well you're just another target for New Labour! We'll see what your image is like after I've put a little spin on it. You'll be drummed out of every church in the country!'

Doctor Spin is on a destructive path. If you can invent and publicize surfball you can invent and publicize anything. Labour Camp may yet develop its own vocabulary of spin. This will be a devious language, very different from the standards of clarity and morality required by George Orwell:

> 'If you simplify your English, you are freed from the worst follies of orthodoxy . . . when you make a stupid remark its stupidity will be obvious, even to yourself. Political language . . . is designed to make lies sound truthful and murder respectable, and to give an appearance of solidity to pure wind. One cannot change all this in a moment, but one can at least change one's own habits.'

On changing habits, I'd like to recommend that Peter Mandelson no longer reads glossy magazines on his exercise bike, but gets a hardback copy of Orwell's *Politics and the English Language* (1946).

Chapter 8

The Country Matters

'There is a strategy of attacking established institutions. When this happens you release destructive power that those institutions had evolved to contain. You release bitterness and anger, not enlightenment and freedom.'

Eric Bettelheim

The logical extension of animal rights is, according to Bertrand Russell, 'votes for oysters'. Animal rights was a term coined in 1975 by an Australian philosopher called Peter Singer. Eric Bettelheim emphasizes the intellectual feebleness of the animal rights lobby when he says 'You must have noticed how the activists tend to be "from the shallow end of the gene pool, espousing a 'philosophy' they can't even spell".'

The country matters in People's Britain, but in a contrary way that illustrates the contradictions and confusions of a culture preoccupied with appearances more than by meaning. The phenomenon of the country – with all its challenges to nostrums about modernizing and about class-based political distinctions – is deeply problematic to Labour Camp. The countryside movement is not a pseudo-event. It may benefit and derive additional force from media attention, but it is authentic, not contrived.

What is New Labour to make of the country? Its inability to cope shows irreconcilable forces within the Party which are scarcely contained under the stylish gloss of Labour Camp. On the one hand, country matters are felt to represent an old order (and very likely 'elitist' too) which should have no influence in the politically correct on-message New Britain being engineered for the People (with the help of Excalibur and focus groups). And by the way, that's 'People' as in city-dwellers and never mind that a good many New-Labour constituencies are suburban territories with a rural periphery which might just yet become radicalized in the style of the countryside movement. So, a democratic movement is ignored. So keen to avoid exclusion in the inner cities, New Labour is merciless about excluding honest countryfolk. At the same time, many of the old Labour anti-hunt activists are reminiscent of the hideous Trotskyite rump which it took Professor Mandelstein and his Modernizers so much time and trouble to purge.

According to Michael Sissons, the literary agent who is an articulate country activist, the anti-hunt lobby has been infiltrated by sinister interests. Animal rights (as opposed to animal welfare, which every decent person supports) is highly politicized. It is an intellectual nonsense, and therefore one of the articles of faith of the dim church of political correctness. It is taught in inner-city schools and is a fashionable cause among uninquisitive youth. At its most extreme, animal rights includes an ultra-Marxist millenarian vision when all animals are returned to a state of primal freedom, and 'speciesism' (to use animal rights activist Richard Ryder's characteristically ugly coinage) is at an end. Never mind that this vision is deluded, philosophically ambiguous, impractical: it is the basis of the anti-hunting movement.

In the dramatically changed circumstances of People's Britain, the stereotype of urban labour versus Tory shires is something of a delusion. Pioneer socialists – one thinks of William Morris, Edward Carpenter and Bernard Shaw, people in tweeds who liked walking – were not exactly strangers to rural ways. Indeed, Morris fled the city to conduct his art and his affairs on the banks of the Thames in Oxfordshire. But stereotypes tend to be enduring and there is a low-brow core even in New Labour that cannot with any ease or comfort accommodate itself to rural issues, whatever they are. Before the 1997 election, people were speculating that if the victory went to Labour, then it would be the first government in British history with no roots in the countryside. Just attempt the mental exercise of imagining any member of New Labour's front bench in a Norfolk jacket to illustrate the precision of this observation. The only attractive members of Labour Camp who (dare) support hunting are John Mortimer (too old to care, too distinguished to be challenged) and Ann Mallalieu (an independent spirit).

The philosophical problem which New Labour has in dealing with the Countryside Movements, capitalized or otherwise, is that it has no credentials in the area. You cannot invent roots and traditions. Cool Britannia was, of course, a misconceived and unsuccessful attempt to buy into a different sort of tradition. No one has yet thought of a pseudo-event that would give New Labour a basis for dealing with a large and extremely disgruntled minority of countryfolk, but in 1945 it had been different: the Labour Government was proud of its rural associations. The wartime Digging for Victory campaign formed an association in the popular imagination between rural work and economic well-being. The Chancellor of the Exchequer, Hugh Dalton, used his first Budget as an appeal to that other delusion, national unity. The farming community was not a hostile contingent of irascible arrogant privileged blood-sporting Tory-voting retards, but a basis for that elusive redemptive formula of one nation. In 1948, Tom Williams, a Minister of Agriculture from a Yorkshire mining community, actually defended blood sports on the basis that it was the privilege of country 'people' to pursue them. Herbert Morrison, Mandelson's grandfather, Clement Attlee, Aneurin Bevan, Ernest Bevin and Hugh Dalton all voted in favour of hunting.

The constituencies of Labour changed during the 1970s and 1980s. Depopulation of the cities and different sources of prosperity dissipated the traditional Labour vote so that the myth of the shoeless beggar woman, her ragged-trouser partner and their starving waif was replaced, at least in part, by semi-educated 'environmental' pressure groups with a menagerie of passionate convictions about fur, whales and foxes. These faunophiliac tendencies did not, of course, extend to fish. The International Fund for Animal Welfare, via its political lobby, gave £1 million to Labour, and until 1996 it paid for a research assistant for Elliot Morley. When Morley was Shadow Minister for Rural Affairs and Animal Welfare, the support from IFAW's lobby group (Political Animal Lobby) appears to have been acknowledged by a pledge to abolish hunting on government-owned land. But overwhelmingly, while the environment was the heraldic banner under which these activists marched, Labour had no articulate spokesman for country affairs, at least as seen by people who lived and worked in the countryside.

Like the Ramblers Association which derives its support from the suburbs, what interest Labour took in the countryside was sourced from urban pressure groups. Like organizing anti-hunt demonstrations, rambling is an urban and suburban occupation, unknown to genuine countryfolk (who would usually rather drive). The Ramblers Association is hilariously housed in an old Barclays Bank building smack in the middle of London's most sulphurous and diabolical intersection: Vauxhall Cross. Here a hundred thousand cars and only slightly fewer bus routes cross every day. The merest attempt to ramble from Ramblers' HQ would result in a massacre of the anoraks. Yet still, on weekends, you can occasionally see bemused groups of urban backpackers – no doubt dreaming about the risible and impertinent 'right to roam' – with celluloid-covered OS maps plotting a route past the famous transvestite pub next to the motorcycle school under Vauxhall railway bridge. Thus the intellectual ferment in which one aspect of Labour's countryside policy is formed.

But in the approach to the 1997 election, Elliott Morley was keen to give assurances to nervous enthusiasts for most country sports. Hunting was isolated because it was considered an easy political target which would find few articulate defenders on any side. Yet, Michael Sissons explains, in characterizing his opponents as 'yobs and slobs' Morley won new friends and exposed a nagging hypocrisy of Labour Camp: the cordons of political correctness do not extend to defend this way off-message minority.

The countryside movement is a genuine democratic movement which New Labour has neither the culture to understand nor the vision to accommodate. While the Prime Minister, who is said to have difficulty recognizing some junior ministers, has no time for Elliott Morley's rabble-rousing, only Robin Cook, Lord Irvine and Jack Straw have presented a feasible means for New Labour addressing a very large and rebellious minority. But even though these individuals are by no means retiring in the presentation of their views, they have neglected the opportunity to be energetically articulate in defence of country interests. That would be off-message. Way off-message too was that huge demonstration of disaffection which the popular country marches on the capital represented.

To a resident of New Labour Camp like advertising man Barry Delaney, the fact that no single message about the countryside was articulated by the marchers indicates that no coherent message exists. But very possibly to an adman, complex and diverse messages involving deep-rooted philosophical issues which cannot be reduced to bites, or given the slick benefits of spin, or condensed into thirty video seconds, or stuck on a forty-eight-sheet poster, may as well not exist. No one outside Labour Camp doubts that the rally on 1st March 1998 contained a total of about half a million people with a silent but very articulate message indeed. Non-verbal communication, it is called. This is the type that defies Excalibur, cannot be spun and resists pseudo-events. No one outside Labour Camp doubts that here is an extraordinary cross-section of the rural population with genuine and heartfelt grievances. There has never been such a popular demonstration in Britain.

Faced with such a broad church of dissidence, New Labour has gone for a political adaptation of Seamus Heaney's 'Whatever you say, say nothing.' In the absence of any intelligent strategy for the countryside, because there is no understanding of what the countryside means, because they arrogantly ignored the smaller rallies that preceded the main event, the best New Labour can do is ignore the whole complex of issues. The countryside is being discredited, but not replaced. Decent, community-minded people are being excluded and the intricate fabric of their lives ignored where it is not actually threatened.

Here is the hypocrisy exposed: the issue for residents of the countryside is the erosion of rural life. The hunting issue has powerful symbolic significance for each side. To the animal rights lobby it is a matter of political correctness. To country people it is a question of the management of the country being taken away from those who know it best. But the debate goes beyond simple matters of agreement or disagreement about field sports. The real issue of the countryside is of immense philosophical significance, and New Labour shows no inclination to deal with it.

The People's Government scorns the identity and integrity of individuals. Even more fundamentally, ignorance of the countryside suggests psychological denial of themes of real note such as wilderness, life and death. A focus group could scarcely come to terms with *thanatos*, or with a rationalization of the Manichean conflicting instincts of destruction and procreation. Freud understood that life might only be fully understood in the context of death. These are maybe not matters routinely debated in The River Café This is an unpalatable notion for a regime consumed by the superficial aspects of image, of celebrity parties and books with jackets by Damien Hirst.

Of course, landscape is a potent national symbol, a genuine shared inheritance if ever there was one. Wrote Richard Hooker in *The Laws of Ecclesiastical Piety* 'See we not plainly that obedience of creatures unto the law of nature is the stay of the whole world?' You don't have to be a backward-looking fat-arsed Tory bigot with a Range Rover and a horsebox (speaking personally I most certainly am not) to appreciate that veneration of the country as both a functional natural resource and as a source of spiritual nutrition is one of the fundamental components of that unique mixture of the utilitarian and the poetic which we (but not the Secretary of State) recognize as 'British Culture'. In Coleridge's beautiful words:

> **'The love of Nature is ever returned double to us . . . by linking our sweetest, but of themselves perishable feelings to distinct and vivid images, which . . . a thousand casual recollections recall to our memory.'**
> (*Anima Poetae*, from the unpublished Notebooks, edited by Ernest Hartley Coleridge)

Yet the people who maintain the countryside are treated as a persecuted minority. This will result in country people becoming what in the US they call Single-Issue Voters, such as the gun lobby. There is a unique relationship in Britain between the land and culture. In the United States, each state returns two Senators so South Dakota has as much representation as New York. In contrast, urban New Labour backbenchers (many of whom have never actually met any examples of the Tory bigots they so energetically despise) have a disproportionate influence on lives and communities they do not understand.

The anti-hunting activists are an ugly mixture of old-fashioned class warfare and demented militant animal rights activists. The topic under discussion is not kindly animal-lovers, but brutish and ruthless political operators. It is curious to note that the founders of the RSPCA in 1824 included some masters of foxhounds, but since 1983 the activists in the RSPCA have been agitating to change the Society's charitable status so that they can be more overtly political.

That move was dropped, although the politicization has continued, so much so that the Charity Commissioners have become alarmed at some of the RSPCA's more loopy and contradictory positions. Some say the RSPCA presents itself dishonestly. And, of course, so does Labour Camp. The RSPCA certainly *behaves* as if it is a political party rather than a charity and refuses membership to those it feels are not ideologically pure. Or 'off-message'.

The Countryside Alliance has the potential to become a genuinely radical movement, a political party with an authentic basis in a popular cause. Its future campaigning will be in those very urban communities which have a rural periphery. Describing New Labour's complacent negligence about rural issues, Eric Bettelheim says:

> **'There is a strategy of attacking established institutions. When this happens you release destructive forces that those institutions had evolved to contain. You release bitterness and anger, not enlightenment and freedom.'**

Such is the potential of Labour's failure on the countryside. Genuine courage and style would produce a culture that defended the values of the country as energetically as it advanced urban causes. Any meaningful vision of Britain must include a vigorous landscape uncontaminated – in letter and spirit – by urban issues. The countryside dilemma exposes the moral emptiness beneath the gloss of Labour Camp and proves how empty is its claim to represent the People.

Chapter 9

River Café
Culture

'Authentic style is the feather in the arrow, not the feather in the cap.'

'Mandy', I was recently told, 'likes his risotto.' We used to have Bollinger Bolsheviks. Now we have rice radicals. Furniture has played its part in the cultural history of New Labour and so too have restaurants. But I wonder if Mandy knows which three varieties of rice (arborio, carnaroli and vialone nano) are favoured in the making of it? My own suspicion is that, if it might win a few points in the polls, Mandy would abandon *cucina casalinga* and go for some terrine of freshly clubbed baby seal washed down with a pint or two of cool virgin's blood.

The Labour Camp is full of contradictions which would discomfort more honest and less arrogant politicians. Who was not stunned to see Melvyn Bragg's athletic reversal of position *vis-à-vis* the Millennium Dome? Bragg's opening stance on Greenwhich had long been signalled by a long, nasal whine about 'arts' funding being neglected in favour of what he believed to be a futile extravagance. But then preferment was suddenly on the agenda. The speed of the Bragg's cynical re-alignment left a dizzy after-image. Bragg (reputed once to have been the recipient of Gore Vidal's stinging put-down 'The trouble with you is you've spent too much time with stupid people', and indisputably the author of lines like '"Again please", you said, and drew me in') has been a consistently articulate and energetic advocate of the arts lobby. As such he has been a stern critic of the Dome as an expensive and unwanted political advertisement when theatre, opera, ballet and so and on are underfunded and neglected. Less than a week after his ascension to the Lords as a 'working' peer was announced, we had Lord Bragg of The Ivy proclaiming his conversion to the Dome cause on BBC Radio 4's lunchtime programme, *The World at One*. The fastidious squirmed.

While Gerry 'Granada' Robinson, the caterer to Nescafé Society, and the man who is going to introduce portion-control aesthetics into the Arts Council, presides over a commercial empire which shovels tons of bad chips and grey burgers into the motoring proletariat in the vilest imaginable surroundings, the cultural policy of New Labour is in fact debated in a handful of London restaurants, especially the ones Lord Bragg likes to visit.

First that comes to mind is The Ivy (0171 836 4751), a Covent Garden landmark. Suffice to say that The Ivy was an old showbiz restaurant and . . . well, perhaps not so much has changed (except the definition of showbusiness which now has to include media-friendly politicians reading scripts provided by the Ministry of Soundbites). As I call to mind a typical Ivy lunchtime scene, what a fine sight I have before me. From my table (and I am not making this up, although memory is, of course, sequential and cumulative) I can see David Puttnam importantly reading a script. John Mortimer, at his favourite corner table, is beckoning to Stephen Daldry, on his favourite booth banquette. Next to me is Joanna Mackle who, as publishing director of Faber & Faber, must claim some responsibility for Chris Smith's atrocious book. She is lunching with Caroline Michel, wife of Faber's *bien pensant* friend-of-Rushdie chairman, Matthew Evans. Melvyn, tie loosened, looking hot, fusses in.

But best of all, the most wonderful exhibit in this menagerie of fine, powerful and influential political animals is the table which accommodates Peter Mandelson and William Sieghart. This lovely pair constitute a resonant coupling indeed. Mandy we have already met. Sieghart is the owner of Forward Publishing which specializes in doing customer magazines for the luxury trade – Patek Philippe Swiss watches and Lexus Japanese cars are clients – but, since everything except the plates has to spin in The Ivy, Sieghart likes to call his business a 'publishing agency'. That is much, much more Labour Camp. We assume he is talking to Mandy in either iambic pentameters or blank verse, since Sieghart's claim to notoriety is sponsorship of the Forward Poetry Prize. I don't know where the old establishment lunches, but it is fascinating to watch the mechanical engineering of the New Establishment in grisly action. On this occasion I left the restaurant in company with the then cheerily embattled Minister for the Arts, Mark Fisher. I told him about this book and said, lightheartedly enough, that it was not my intention to bring down the government. Fisher, a man of substance and integrity, then having predictable difficulty getting himself taken seriously, looked disappointed. He was soon sacked.

Then there is Granita in Islington's Upper Street (0171 278 0219). It was here, perhaps over a little salad of red oak leaf, shredded Gruyère and croutons, that Gordon Brown famously conceded leadership that fateful night of 31st May 1994 and old Labour was, in an environment of harsh furniture, forever after translated into New. Thus, in the holy writ of New Labour, Granita has an iconic position comparable in its way to the role of the Deux Magots in the development and popular perception of Parisian existentialism. One day it will have an English Heritage Blue Plaque. Drama-documentaries will be made here. In the meantime, things have quietened down: since Tony and Cherie left Barnsbury on the night of 2nd May 1997, Upper Street is no longer on the flight path of New Labour.

Supremely, there is The River Café (0171 381 8824). If New
Labour has a scriptural home it is surely here. The only negative
thing it is possible to say about The River Café is that it is on the
flight path to Heathrow. It is not true that The River Café *invented*
Italian cooking, but you could be mistaken for thinking so. To be a
bitch, The River Café did not even invent its own name: Brooklyn
had one nearly twenty years ago. The restaurant, run by Ruth, the
wife of Richard Rogers (and originally intended as his staff
canteen), and Rose Gray, has reached such critical status that any
negative comment hints at betrayal of a cause, a blasphemy. It
would be almost Politically Incorrect to comment adversely on its
environment and its trademark dishes (seared butterfly leg of
lamb with *salsa verde*) which, in their robust simplicity, articulate
a conception of quality – and, indeed, deliver a taste – which is
beyond the flashy, trashy, image-conscious political jostlings of so
many of members of the restaurant's customer base. The Great
Exhibition of 1851 was memorably described by Andrew St
George in his book *The Descent of Manners* (1993) as a
'sparkling network of connection and inter-relation', a description
that will do very nicely for The River Café which is a Great
Exhibition all of its own. The BBC's Alan Yentob, a pilot fish of
New Labour, has been seen here more than once.

Let us explore this sparkling network of connection and inter-
relation a little. The pilot fish Yentob is a colleague of John Birt.
Yentob holidays in those parts of Tuscany also favoured by the
Prime Minister, while Birt knew Peter Mandelson when each
was working at London Weekend Television in the early
eighties. Later Mandelson worked for the market research
consultancy SRU, founded by Sir Denis Stevenson who became

a Trustee of the Tate Gallery in 1988 (and subsequently its Chairman). That classic pseudo-event, The Turner Prize, is a feature of Yentob's arts programming and came to public prominence during Stevenson's period of influence at the Tate. It was the same Millbank gallery that was the scene of the launch party of Chris Smith's book, *Creative Britain*, whose cover was designed by Damien Hirst, a winner of the Turner Prize. *Creative Britain* was published by the distinguished old house of Faber whose editorial director was Robert McCrum until he was laid low by a stroke, from which he has now happily recovered. McCrum bought Salman Rushdie's old house in Islington when the novelist went into hiding. Ruth Rogers, who cooks at The River Café, used to attend parties in aid of Rushdie's rehabilitation and McCrum's recuperation was greatly accelerated by superb meals sent around to his hospital room from the River Café kitchens. It was at the launch of the second edition of *The River Café Cookbook* that I was personally introduced to Bob Ayling, Chief Executive of British Airways, who was also a guest. Ayling is the Chairman of the New Millennium Experience Company whose architect is the proprietor of The River Café. The proprietor of The River Café is, of course, Lord Rogers of Riverside whose colleague, Philip Gumuchdjian, is the architect who designed Lord Puttnam's boathouse in County Cork. Lord Rogers' publishers are Faber whose Chairman is Matthew Evans, a director of The Groucho Club. This sparkling network is the framework of a very hermetic new establishment, as exclusive and as excluding as the one we thought we'd got rid of so long ago.

Of course, for people who believe architecture and food are

paramount in civilized society (for people like me, in fact), for
people who find the clutter and squalor of the world intolerable,
The River Café offers some sort of deliverance. Architecture and
good food share a basis in morality, style and function. You need a
decent concept and excellent materials to achieve either a good
building design or a delicious dish. A building should be functional
and a recipe must be nutritious. Buildings and food should also
look good. The River Café achieves each with a breezy air of
minimalist hedonism that is deceptively facile. It's a truly great
restaurant (if not quite, as *The New Yorker* suggested, 'the best
Italian restaurant in the world'– amusingly parodied by A. A. Gill as
'the best Fulham restaurant in the world').

But in the interests of the forensic analysis of style as opposed to
substance which is meant to be the keynote of this little book, let's
try a moment's dissent about The River Café just for the sake of
polemic. The River Café was not the first place to offer little bowls
of extra virgin olive oil for dipping *ciabatta*: Orso was doing it more
than three years earlier. Like William Morris' wholesome vision of
handicraft (which was so expensive as to be beyond the reach of all
but the very rich) the vernacular populism of The River Café is
something of a deception. It has the sort of simplicity it costs a
fortune to achieve. It is also expensive and exclusive. And while the
cooking is superb, it is not without elements of authoritarianism all
its own. The gastronomic programme is a rigid and inflexible one: if
you believe that a restaurant of quality is the type that would serve
you a jam sandwich if that was what you ordered, The River Café
would not qualify. And as for being *authentically* Italian, that's a very
vexatious issue. I think if you took someone from Reggio da
Calabria to Rainville Road, he'd identify as few of the dishes on the

menu as 'authentic' as would someone from Novara exposed to the same gastronomic experiment. The River Café (and this is part of its genius) has created a synthetic Italian *cucina* that transcends mere comparison with the untidy regionality of Italy itself, where beans and steak are available in Tuscany but rare in the Veneto where polenta is a staple. In Piedmont and Lombardy risotto is commonplace and spaghetti exotic.

The phenomenal popularity of Italian food is a noteworthy feature of transatlantic culture, but is it curmudgeonly to wonder how long this esteem may last and is it equally curmudgeonly to make a comparison between some aspects of Labour Camp and some aspects of The River Café? The site and style of the restaurant are in some way revealing of a deeper truth. It is in Hammersmith, but not the gritty dogshit-and-diesel part of Hammersmith, rather in the quietly genteel backroads of the Borough. Thus it avoids the stigma of being too exclusively metropolitan while at the same time being emphatically urban: you cannot, for instance, imagine under any circumstances the leaders of Labour Camp collectivizing in a country house hotel no matter how many varieties of risotto were on the *carta*.

In matters of style, The River Café is the rhetoric of Labour Camp made flash and flesh. Architecturally, it is incontrovertibly modern (but housed in an antique shell). It is apparently busy and popular, but the constituency is in fact a privileged elite. Gastronomically, the cooking tends towards a process that Fay Maschler, the restaurant critic, beautifully described as interference with raw materials up to the point of transformation, but no further. A more perceptive criticism of

Government policies could not be articulated. They, too, aim to reach the point of transformation, but to go no further. The reputations of both The River Café and of New Labour depend on adroit deceptions cheerfully absorbed with uncritical adulation by a sparkling network of true believers. Dissent, as we said, is not allowed. It would spoil the party.

In 1964 Susan Sontag could list the following items as a part of the 'Canon of Camp' (*Notes on Camp*). Some are unrecognizable today, but to convey the period charm I will reproduce the list in full and add a little parenthetic gloss.

Zuleika Dobson
        (the heroine of Max Beerbohm's cult Oxford novel)
Scopitone films
        (a coin-operated French visual jukebox of 1963,
        precursor of rock videos; showed 16mm colour shorts
        of Lesley Gore, Dion, Nancy Sinatra and the Tijuana
        Brass; redundant by 1968)
The Brown Derby Restaurant on Sunset Boulevard in LA
        (landmark of Californian vernacular kitsch, ironically ele-
        vated into a Post-Modern monument by Charles Jencks)
The Enquirer, headlines and stories
        (trailer trash supermarket checkout rag)
Aubrey Beardsley drawings
        (decadent masterpieces of erotic Art Nouveau)
Swan Lake
        (balletomanic Tchaikovski)
Bellini's opera
        (just then being rediscovered)

Visconti's direction of *Salome* and *'Tis Pity She's a Whore*
       (butch Italian historicism)
Certain turn-of-the-century postcards
       (nostalgic kitsch)
Schoedsack's *King Kong*
       (Ernest B. Schoedsack was, with Merlin C. Cooper, a
       director of the 1933 classic)
The Cuban pop singer La Lupe
       (defunct salsa star of 1960s and 1970s)
Lynn Ward's novel in woodcuts, *God's Man*
       (published in 1929, subsequently subject of a camp
       revival)
The old Flash Gordon comics
       (prototypical pop culture of the 1930s)
Women's clothes of the 1920s (feather boas, fringed and
beaded dresses, etc.)
       (flapping regally out of the dressing-up box)
The novels of Ronald Firbank and Ivy Compton Burnett
       (effete classics)
Stag movies seen without lust
       (characteristic Camp sensibility)

Too literal a reinterpretation of Sontag's original 'Canon of Camp'
would be heavy-handed, but the comparisons thirty-five years on
are endless. Labour Camp has a canon all of its own. What this
canon lacks is wit and honesty. Labour Camp is based on a
number of deceptions, disguised by a ham-fisted and poorly
judged reliance on the most superficial aspects of style. The
rotten intellectual catastrophe here is the misunderstanding of
style itself: genuine style arises from profound beliefs, expressed

with unforced wit, restless energy and uncontaminated sincerity. Labour Camp relies on deception and manipulation.

In any discussion of how modern governments present popular ideas, The Great Exhibition of 1851 always comes to mind as an exemplar against whose success all its successors must be judged. It donated much to modern life: it was a genuinely popular mass event which left behind a distinctive heritage. The Victoria & Albert Museum, to name only one tangible for instance, was filled with the surplus the Exhibition's Commissioners found left on their hands. While The Great Exhibition was emphatically not a pseudo-event, it did have its celebrities. Not only Prince Albert and Henry Cole, of course, but also the designer of the structure, Joseph Paxton. It was not only a great building design which Paxton contributed to world culture, but also a heroic moral exemplar. Having risen from a humble foreman to a figure of international prominence, Paxton both expressed and directed the High Victorian belief in social progress. His advancement through hard work and genius would have satisfied Samuel Smiles, author of the original auto-improvement manual, *Self Help* (1859). If there are moralists in Labour Camp, they have not yet come forward to be identified. Still less is there anyone of Albert's, Cole's or Paxton's stature.

Many of the smug elite munching *cucina casalinga* in The River Café or chewing thoughtfully on fishcakes at The Ivy would – one imagines – cite William Morris as a moral exemplar, as a spiritual precedent for the revolution they have created. But how much of the Labour Camp can bear Morris' severe test:

'In my mind, it is not possible to dissociate art from morality, politics and religion.'

If Morris had known that under New Labour art, morality and politics were mired by advertising and public relations, he would have been appalled. Labour Camp is not about the triumph of style over substance, but about its failure. Here are people who do not seem to understand that authentic style is the feather in the arrow, not the feather in the cap. It shows that the professional communications businesses are influencing politics, just as politics is attempting to influence art. Advertising itself grew from a primitive period when it was concerned with *claims* to a more sophisticated one when it communicated *images*. It moved from bare facts to persuasion. The big challenge in future is to reverse this trend.

Postscript

Millennium Muddle 2

'One imagines a focus group would very likely have turned down the Great Pyramid (impractical), Beethoven's late quartets (too difficult) and Guernica (too inflammatory).'

An unsent open letter to the Prime Minister 1997

The decision to celebrate the Millennium is right: a stylish, audacious and unexpected decision by the new government. The British have an idiosyncratic genius in organizing unlikely activities exceptionally well, as 1851 and 1951 demonstrated. The Crystal Palace gave Britain 'ownership' of taste while the Festival of Britain was a symbol of national revival, evidently unforgettable to any visitor.

Great exhibitions have the power to motivate and to educate. Many of the products which characterise this century – electric light, the lift and the telephone, for instance – were demonstrated for the first time in international exhibitions. Even more significantly, the great architectural innovations and styles, from the Garden City movement to systems building, via Art Nouveau, Art Deco and Modernism itself, were first seen in exhibitions. The New York World's Fair of 1938 brought industrial design to international attention and, incidentally, attracted 45 million visitors. Now that computerized inter-activity is a domestic commonplace, the exhibition can re-invent itself as a unique medium which engages the public in that fascinating area halfway between entertainment and education. There is a great heritage for a Millennium exhibition to build on.

Of course the Greenwich project has its critics, but a degree of scepticism is inevitable and healthy for so visible a public undertaking. There are those who criticize the site as remote and inaccessible, but this is a spurious argument. If there is good reason, people will come. Some question the building itself as costly and impractical, but Richard Rogers' tent is an ingenious and economical design. Everyone is rightly concerned about the enormous expense. Indeed, while narrow definitions of profitability are inappropriate for a venture with a serious educational dimension, the nation can get real value from a Millennium Experience of genuine quality.

There is a compelling argument for celebrating the Millennium here in London. This city is the creative capital of the planet. For architects, designers, artists, directors, writers, musicians and photographers there is nowhere better to work. And by no means all are ethnically British, just one reason why the Union Jack argument is irrelevant: the fact is that the world's biggest Millennium event is happening in London. That's enough in itself. We have global data traffic, instantaneous capital international transfer of capital. Old-fashioned interpretations of nationhood are inappropriate: people want and need to be in London. Companies too: Volvo, for instance, may move its headquarters here. The capital's creative energy and resources are a priceless national asset, especially so in the Information Age when ideas and images have become even more valuable than manufactured goods.

The opportunity exists – or perhaps rather *existed* because it may now be too late – to make Greenwich a comprehensive showcase for talent and expertise: something entertaining, informative as well as a persuasive, a very visible international demonstration of that British idiosyncratic genius. Given the associations of the Millennium and Greenwich with time, the entire 'experience' should be about the future. To have the best architects and designers presenting a tangible vision of the 'place we are all going to live' would not only become an attraction of compelling popular interest, it would be immediately comprehensible to the (sometimes baffled) media and, most significantly, relevant to all the sponsors on which the project's finances depend.

One of the defining characteristics of the contemporary age is that, in the words of the great Italian designer Ettore Sottsass Jnr, 'industry does not have to buy culture, because today industry *is* culture'. Sottsass meant that there is no need for, say, Ford to sponsor an opera to give it cultural credentials because its cars already have a legitimate claim to being late-twentieth-century culture in their own right.

It's in this spirit that sponsors should be involved in the Millennium: not as short-term tenants of a pavilion, but as partners and collaborators mapping the future for the public's consideration and comment. Thus, Ford would show us the car of the future, Sainsbury's the shop of the future, Microsoft the library of the future, while Guinness would explain if we are still going to be using pubs (or even actually drinking) in 2051. All of this could be achieved at a reasonable cost.

It is this sense of privileged insight, almost of voyeurism, that makes exhibitions stimulating. A collaboration between government, industry and the public which used the Dome as a vast laboratory of culture, technology and taste would amply satisfy the requirements of all parties and leave a vivid legacy of ideas. If visitors to the Millennium know more about current thinking on the future, then they are better able to influence it. The

Millennium Experience should be a confident expression of a vision, based on superb academic research, supported by sponsors who are cultural and technical collaborators, not merely sources of funds, and executed with uncompromising bravura by the very best architects, artists, film-makers, musicians, writers and designers.

But instead of clear vision and courage, there is a bias towards reactive expediency. Of course, it is inevitable that there should be a political dimension to a government-funded project, but it is ruinous if this dominates – especially so when the political context is fuelled by a constant drip from focus groups. Consumer research is no substitute for creative decision-making.

Great works of architecture, art and design can never be tested by focus groups and nor should they be momentarily adjusted to meet the latest lurch of opinion polls. The same goes for exhibitions. It's worth emphasizing that, so far, the unique symbol of the Millennium – Richard Rogers' famous Dome – is itself a bold creative gesture, ironically designed without reference to focus groups, market research or opinion polls. As with all Lord Rogers' buildings, it is a bloody-minded insistence on knowing best. Quite right too.

One imagines a focus group would very likely have turned down the Great Pyramid (impractical), Beethoven's late quartets (too difficult) and Guernica (too inflammatory). The Egyptians, Beethoven and Picasso were all prepared to think the unthinkable. That's the nature of creativity and we are all very grateful they were so pig-headedly unreasonable. Alas, in a culture which encourages feeble-minded political correctness, great monuments and great works of art are not to be anticipated.

The influence of opinion-adjusted political correctness threatens to move the Millennium towards trivia. Greenwich should not attempt to replicate a Florida theme park: that would be an unworthy and lowering catastrophe. Disney is excellent, but has far more resources and experience: it has taken Disney nearly fifty years to establish its prodigious expertise. Besides, why go to a pale, thin imitation of Disney when the real thing is just three hours from London by train? Nor should the Millennium be like a rock concert or a West End show. We do those things very well already – and they cost much, much less money.

My advice is simple. Since the Millennium depends on creative excellence to succeed, the big decisions about the content should be made by suitably qualified creative individuals unimpaired by political considerations, still less *party* political ones. The contents need the same style, audacity and unexpectedness that characterized the decision to carry on with the original project.

There is a simple and elegant solution to the vexatious question of the Dome's contents. The best architects and designers in the world, in technical partnership with the world's great companies, should present a challenging vision of the future. An exhibition of world-historical importance could be created for a fraction of the fortune presently being considered. A clearer idea and reduced costs would bring about an impressive gain. Now *there's* a stimulating idea for the future!

Appendix

Here is a summary of the great international exhibitions which the Millennium Dome now joins. The artistic and intellectual achievements of Labour Camp will be judged in this context.

Paris 1798
The Exposition de l'Industrie, held in the Champ de Mars, was the very first realization of the international exhibition idea. France's new revolutionary government in 1798 wanted to restore interest in neglected national economic assets, including Sèvres, Gobelins and Savonnerie. There were 110 exhibitors in all. By 1849 and the eleventh exhibition in the same series, the number of exhibitors had risen to 4,500 and the exhibition had become an established feature of contemporary economic and cultural life.

London 1851
It is almost impossible even to form a melodramatic estimate of the extent of the influence or significance of The Great Exhibition of the Works of Industry of all Nations, although it may be worth pointing out that not all anticipations were favourable. The King of Prussia forebade his relatives to visit London because he feared socialists would foregather in Kensington Gardens. Locally, there were fears that the crowds would excite a revival of the Black Death and that the first strong gust would bring the building down. Pugin's Medieval Court was assumed a clandestine promotion for Popery and protectionists argued that the exhibition would suck in undesirable foreign imports. More positively, in an age when manufactured goods dominated economic activity, 1851 demonstrated that London was the world centre of both art and industry (a conceit incorporated into both the philosophical programme of the Albert Memorial and the nearby 'Albert University' which evolved into the Royal College of Art). Besides Joseph Paxton's remarkable building, a world-leader in large-scale prefabrication, the legacy of the Great Exhibition was that 'design' (or 'art and industry', as it was known), became an institution of all advanced cultures.

Paris 1855
The Exposition Universelle des Produits de l'Industrie was inspired by London 1851. There were three essential exhibitions: the Palais de l'Industrie at the southern end of the Champs-Elysées, l'Halle des Machines parallel to the banks of the Seine and an art exhibition just off the Avenue Montaigne. Mid-century France was much less industrialized than Britain and the architecture of the Paris exhibition buildings was less confident than London's (although it covered a larger ground area and, with 5.1 million visitors, was only a little behind London's total of 6 million). The Exposition Universelle introduced the French public to industrialization in general and to aluminium as an industrial and building material in particular. There were nearly 21,000 exhibitors.

Paris 1867
The Exposition Universelle attracted 11 million visitors. Among the 42,217 exhibitors were some of the great innovations in aniline dyes and power turbines.

Philadelphia 1876
The US Centennial Exhibition was vast, covering 175ha, attracting 10.1 million visitors who saw some of the very first mass-produced typewriters and sewing machines. Alexander Graham Bell demonstrated his telephone and Westinghouse his air brake. The press was awed by what they described as a 'mighty cosmos'. The public was awed by the first commercially available banana, foil-wrapped at 10 cents.

Paris 1878
This latest in the series of Expositions Universelles attracted 16 million. On display were some of the first working lifts, telephones, cars, refrigerators and electric street lighting.

Regent Street 1888
Here the first public showing of the Arts and Crafts Exhibition Society was at the New Gallery, Regent Street.

Melbourne 1888–9, Antwerp 1894
If you study the labels of, say, Martini vermouth and Heineken beer, you'll see what an important contribution these exhibitions made to popular culture.

Paris 1889
The Eiffel Tower, the world's greatest city symbol and exhibition building, was designed for the 1889 Exposition. 32.2 million visitors also saw Edison's phonograph. The Eiffel Tower has achieved such resonance not only on account of its daring structure, but because it was the visible evidence and enduring token of an exhibition with memorable contents.

Chicago 1893
The World's Columbian Exhibition (a year behind schedule to celebrate Columbus' arrival in 1492) attracted 27.3 million visitors. Travelators and electric overhead railways were among the exhibits and this was among the very first popular events where electricity was universal. The exhibition was also the first grand essay of Daniel H. Burnham's stolid classical style. The public was entertained by George Washington Ferris's famous wheel.

Paris 1900
Art Nouveau was made public to 50.8 million visitors in the exhibits of Galle, Majorelle, Grasset and Mucha. The museum buildings, especially the Petit Palais and Grand Palais, established Paris as a peerless international exhibition centre.

Paris 1925
The Exposition des Arts Décoratifs et Industriels gave the world the term 'Art Deco', seen in the exhibits of Ruhlmann, Chareau and Lalique. In contrast, Le Corbusier presented his Pavillon de l'Esprit Nouveau, the first absolutely pure essay in Modernism.

Stuttgart 1927
Stuttgart hosted a major housing exhibition organised by the Deustche Werkbund. Mies van der Rohe was Director. The buildings designed and exhibited by Mies and J. J. P. Oud, Mart Stam, Le Corbusier, Peter Behrens and Walter Gropius were the definitive statement of International Modernism. Defining Modern objects and furniture were first seen here too, including chairs by Mies and Mart Stam, Heinz and Bodo Rasch, lights by Poul Henningsen and Marianne Brandt.

Barcelona 1929
For the Exposicion Internacional de Barcelona Mies van der Rohe designed the epochal German Pavilion and the furniture to furnish it (although rather minimal-istically). Designed for temporary ease of the Royal person, the 'Barcelona Chair' became a classic of mid-century Modernism in the service of corporate America.

Chicago 1933–4
A Century of Progress – International Exhibition. 48.7 million visitors saw the first mass-produced televisions. 'Styling' was established as a consumer language.

Paris 1937
34 million visitors came to the Exposition Internationale des Arts et Techniques Appliqués à la Vie Moderne, situated in the new Trocadero which was left behind as Paris's Museum of Modern Art.

New York 1938
The New York World's Fair covered 486ha and attracted 44.9 million visitors. The spectacular exhibition buildings – by Walter Dorwin Teague, among others – reconciled US Styling with European Modernism and created a language of design that would last nearly fifty years. Albert Einstein gave lectures.

London 1951
An exercise literally *designed* to raise the spirits and direct the energies of the country. There were great hopes (inspired by the BoT) that the Festival of Britain would have a stimulating effect on architecture and design, but as Gerald Barry recognized in a 10th anniversary lecture, the Festival was a failure in these terms. The Festival Style (as we now see it) was not influential and lent itself to ignorant travesty. But it's clear that the Festival *did* play its part in developing public taste (a role later taken up by the Council of Industrial Design from 1956 when the Design Centre opened in the Haymarket). The image set before the public by the Festival influenced the style of the Design Centre just as surely as its programme was based on many of the Festival's assumptions about a brighter, more colourful world.

Brussels 1958
Exposition Universelle et Internationale de Bruxelles. First mainland Europe exhibition since the war. 41.4 million visitors. Atomium now a Brussels landmark.

Montreal 1967
Expo '67 attracted 50.3 million visitors. Buckminster Fuller demonstrated his geodesic dome as the US Pavilion. Moshe Safdie's Habitat 67 was an ingenious re-interpretation of Modernist housing principles, intended to break the rigidity of the International Style.

Osaka 1970
Japan's entrance on the world stage as an economic superpower was the Japan World Exposition. Kenzo Tange presented his astonishing space-frame architecture and the 64.2 million visitors also saw futuristic pneumatic buildings which have still not been realized.

Sources

Parts of *Labour Camp* originally appeared in a slightly different form in Esquire, The Daily Telegraph and The Observer. The rest is based on conversations on and off the record with Eric Bettelheim, Sir Terence Conran, Stephen Daldry, Barry Delaney, Sir Philip Dowson, Roy Hattersley, Professor Anthony O' Hear, Chris Powell, Michael Seiffert, Michael Sissons, Sir Roy Strong, John Underwood and others who preferred not to be mentioned.

Besides Susan Sontag's inspiring essay *Notes on Camp* which first appeared in The Partisan Review, New York, 1964, two other important cultural studies were very influential on the thinking behind this book. The first was Hellmut Lehmann-Haupt's *Art Under A Dictatorship*, Oxford University Press, 1954. In this pioneering and superbly researched study Lehmann-Haupt made the striking observation that authoritarian regimes of whatever colour tend to invest in bad art of a similar style. The second was Daniel J. Boorstin's *The Image – or what happened to the American Dream*, Atheneum, New York, 1962, which defined the unforgettable concept of the 'pseudo-event'.

Lord Runciman's diaries were published as an article in The London Review of Books edition of 4th June, 1998. Another recent publication which gives the flavour of the mood in Labour's camp is Nicholas Jones' *Soundbites and Spindoctors*, Cassell, 1995. Jane and Michael Stern's *Encyclopaedia of Pop Culture*, Harper Perennial, New York, 1992, is always besides me whatever I am writing.